Corporate Governance: A Comprehensive Guide

DR. KANGAN SAYAL

DR. NIKHIL MONGA

Dr. NAVDEEP KAUR

First Edition of the book is published in 2023
Published by Kindle Direct Publishing

DEDICATION

This book is dedicated to my parents.

CONTENTS

PREFACE

Corporate governance is a vital aspect of modern business that ensures the effective management, transparency, and accountability of companies. It encompasses a set of principles, processes, and practices that guide the conduct of organizations and their interactions with stakeholders. In an increasingly complex and interconnected business environment, the need for robust corporate governance practices has become more evident than ever.

This book aims to provide a comprehensive understanding of corporate governance, with a specific focus on the Indian context. It explores the legal and regulatory framework that governs corporate governance in India, including the role of key regulatory bodies such as the Securities and Exchange Board of India (SEBI) and the Reserve Bank of India (RBI). The evolution of corporate governance in India is also examined, highlighting the changes and developments that have shaped the landscape of corporate governance in the country.

The role and responsibilities of the board of directors, as the central governing body of a company, are discussed in detail. This includes insights into board composition and structure, the functions of board committees, the significance of independent directors, and the importance of board evaluation and succession planning. The book also delves into the rights and protection of shareholders, shareholder activism, institutional investors, and related party transactions.

Disclosure and transparency, essential pillars of corporate governance, are explored, emphasizing the importance of accurate financial reporting, auditing, and the role of information technology in facilitating transparency. The concept of corporate social responsibility (CSR) reporting and its impact on corporate governance practices is also examined.

Risk management and internal controls receive due attention, addressing the identification and assessment of risks, the establishment of internal control mechanisms, fraud prevention, and the implementation of robust whistleblower mechanisms. The book further explores the relationship between corporate governance and various stakeholders, including employees, customers, suppliers, and the community, highlighting the importance of their engagement and the practice of responsible governance.

Drawing on case studies and best practices, the book showcases exemplary corporate governance initiatives and highlights the challenges faced in implementing effective governance frameworks. It also provides insights into corporate governance ratings, rankings, and the future direction of corporate governance practices in India.

This book is designed to serve as a comprehensive guide for students, professionals, and practitioners seeking to understand and navigate the dynamic landscape of corporate governance in India. It aims to facilitate discussions, promote best practices, and inspire further research in the field. By equipping readers with knowledge and insights, it endeavors to contribute to the advancement of corporate governance and foster a culture of responsible and ethical business practices in India and beyond.

We hope that this book will serve as a valuable resource and inspire readers to actively participate in shaping the future of corporate governance in India, fostering sustainable growth and trust in our business environment.

CHAPTER 1
INTRODUCTION TO CORPORATE GOVERNANCE

Dr. Nikhil Monga[1]

Chapter Abstract

The chapter Introduction to Corporate Governance provides a comprehensive overview of the fundamental concepts and principles of corporate governance. It explores the definition and significance of corporate governance in the modern business landscape, highlighting its role in establishing trust, transparency, and accountability. The chapter introduces key principles of corporate governance, such as accountability, fairness, transparency, independence, and responsibility.

1. What is Corporate Governance

Corporate governance refers to the system of rules, practices, and processes by which a company is directed, controlled, and managed. It encompasses the relationships and interactions between various stakeholders, such as shareholders, management, board of directors, employees, customers, suppliers, and the broader community. The primary goal of corporate governance is to ensure that a company operates in a transparent, accountable, and responsible manner, while protecting the interests of its shareholders and stakeholders.

Corporate governance sets the framework for decision-making and ensures that the interests of shareholders and stakeholders are balanced and safeguarded. It establishes a system of checks and balances to prevent conflicts of interest, mismanagement, fraud, and other unethical practices. By providing a structure for effective oversight and control, corporate

---

[1] Professor, School of Management Studies, CT University, Ludhiana

governance promotes long-term sustainability, ethical behavior, and value creation.

1.1 Definitions of Corporate Governance

Corporate governance can be defined in several ways, depending on the perspective and context. Here are three commonly used definitions of corporate governance:

The Organization for Economic Cooperation and Development (OECD) Definition:

"The system by which companies are directed and controlled. Boards of directors are responsible for the governance of their companies. The shareholders' role in governance is to appoint the directors and auditors and to satisfy themselves that an appropriate governance structure is in place. The responsibilities of the board include setting the company's strategic aims, providing the leadership to put them into effect, supervising the management of the business, and reporting to shareholders on their stewardship."

The Cadbury Report Definition:

"Corporate governance is the system by which companies are directed and controlled. Boards of directors are responsible for the governance of their companies. The shareholders' role in governance is to appoint the directors and the auditors and to satisfy themselves that an appropriate governance structure is in place. The responsibilities of the board include setting the company's strategic aims, providing the leadership to put them into effect, supervising the management of the business, and reporting to shareholders on their stewardship."

The International Finance Corporation (IFC) Definition:

"Corporate governance is the system by which companies are directed and controlled. It involves a set of relationships between a company's management, its board, its shareholders, and other stakeholders. Corporate governance provides the structure through which the objectives of the company are set, and the means of attaining those objectives and monitoring performance are determined."

The European Commission Definition:

"Corporate governance refers to the system through which companies are directed and controlled. It involves a set of relationships between a company's management, its board, its shareholders, and other stakeholders. Corporate governance provides the structure through which the objectives of the company are set, and the means of attaining those objectives and monitoring performance are determined."

The World Bank Definition:

"Corporate governance refers to the way in which companies are governed and controlled, encompassing the relationships among a company's management, its board, its shareholders, and other stakeholders. Effective corporate governance structures encourage companies to create value and provide accountability and control systems commensurate with the risks involved."

These definitions highlight the role of boards of directors, the importance of shareholder rights and responsibilities, and the relationship between management, shareholders, and other stakeholders in the governance process. Corporate governance aims to establish mechanisms that ensure effective decision-making, transparency, accountability, and the protection of shareholders' interests while considering the broader stakeholder ecosystem.

2. Evolution of Corporate Governance in India

The evolution of corporate governance in India has been a significant journey marked by various reforms and developments. India recognized the importance of effective corporate governance practices to attract investments, protect shareholder interests, and foster sustainable economic growth. Let's delve into the key milestones and transformations in the evolution of corporate governance in India.

2.1 The Confederation of Indian Industry (CII) Code (1998): In 1998, the Confederation of Indian Industry (CII) released a voluntary code of corporate governance, known as the CII Code. It laid down principles and best practices for corporate governance, including transparency, accountability, and protection of shareholder rights. The CII Code played a crucial role in creating awareness and initiating the corporate governance discourse in India.

2.2 The Kumar Mangalam Birla Committee Report (2000): The Kumar Mangalam Birla Committee Report, constituted by the Securities and Exchange Board of India (SEBI), was a significant milestone in India's corporate governance journey. The report emphasized the need for independent directors, audit committees, and improved financial disclosures. It recommended several reforms, including the separation of roles of chairman and managing director, to enhance corporate governance practices.

2.3 The SEBI Clause 49 (2000 and subsequent amendments): SEBI, the regulatory body for securities markets in India, introduced Clause 49 as part of the Listing Agreement in 2000. It mandated certain corporate governance practices for listed companies in India. Key provisions included the composition and role of independent directors, audit committees, and disclosures on related party transactions. Over the years, SEBI has made several amendments to Clause 49 to strengthen corporate governance norms, aligning them with international best practices.

2.4 The Companies Act, 2013: The Companies Act, 2013, marked a significant milestone in the evolution of corporate governance in India. The

Act introduced comprehensive reforms to enhance transparency, accountability, and shareholder rights. Key provisions included the establishment of National Company Law Tribunal (NCLT) and National Company Law Appellate Tribunal (NCLAT) for faster resolution of corporate disputes, mandatory rotation of auditors, and greater emphasis on independent directors and board effectiveness.

2.5 The Kotak Committee Report (2018): In 2017, SEBI constituted a committee headed by Uday Kotak to review and improve corporate governance standards. The Kotak Committee Report made several recommendations, including strengthening the role of independent directors, enhancing disclosures on governance practices, and reducing the maximum number of directorships held by individuals. SEBI implemented many of these recommendations through amendments to Listing Regulations, further advancing corporate governance practices in India.

2.6 Corporate Social Responsibility (CSR) Requirements: The Companies Act, 2013, also introduced mandatory CSR provisions for certain companies. This required companies to allocate a portion of their profits towards social and environmental initiatives. This move emphasized the role of companies in addressing societal needs and promoting responsible business practices.

2.7 Stewardship Code: In 2020, SEBI introduced the Stewardship Code, which outlines the responsibilities of institutional investors, such as mutual funds and insurance companies, in promoting good corporate governance practices. The Stewardship Code encourages institutional investors to actively engage with companies, exercise their voting rights, and participate in governance-related activities.

Overall, the evolution of corporate governance in India has witnessed a shift towards greater transparency, accountability, and shareholder protection. The reforms and developments have aimed to align Indian corporate governance practices with international standards and best practices, fostering investor confidence and sustainable business growth. Continuous efforts are being made to further strengthen corporate governance mechanisms and promote a culture of responsible and ethical business conduct in India.

3. Principles of Corporate Governance

The principles of corporate governance serve as guiding principles and best practices that help organizations establish effective governance frameworks. These principles provide a foundation for responsible management, accountability, transparency, and the protection of stakeholders' interests. While specific principles may vary slightly across jurisdictions and frameworks, there are several widely recognized principles of corporate governance. Here are some of the key principles:

3.1 Accountability: Accountability is a fundamental principle of corporate governance. It involves ensuring that individuals, particularly directors and executives, are responsible for their actions and decisions. Accountability requires transparency in reporting, adherence to laws and regulations, and the ability to justify and explain decisions to stakeholders.

3.2 Transparency: Transparency refers to the openness and accessibility of information related to the company's activities, financial performance, and governance practices. Transparent reporting ensures that stakeholders have access to accurate, timely, and relevant information to make informed decisions. This includes financial reporting, disclosure of non-financial information, and transparency in decision-making processes.

3.3 Fairness: The principle of fairness emphasizes treating all stakeholders in a fair and equitable manner. Fairness involves ensuring that the rights and interests of shareholders, employees, customers, suppliers, and other stakeholders are respected and protected. Fairness also includes impartiality in decision-making processes and avoiding conflicts of interest.

3.4 Independence: Independence is a crucial principle in corporate governance. It emphasizes the need for independent oversight and decision-making to prevent undue influence or conflicts of interest. Independence is often achieved through the presence of independent directors on the board, independent audit committees, and independent external auditors.

3.5 Responsibility: Responsibility entails the recognition that companies have a broader responsibility beyond maximizing shareholder value. It involves considering the social, environmental, and economic impacts of business activities and taking actions to contribute positively to society. Responsible governance practices integrate environmental, social, and governance (ESG) factors into decision-making processes.

3.6 Board Effectiveness: Board effectiveness refers to the ability of the board of directors to fulfill its responsibilities and drive the organization's success. Effective boards have a diverse composition, including independent directors with relevant expertise and experience. They possess a clear understanding of their roles and responsibilities, actively engage in strategic decision-making, and provide constructive oversight of management.

3.7 Risk Management: Effective risk management is a key principle of corporate governance. It involves identifying, assessing, and managing risks to protect the organization's assets, reputation, and long-term sustainability. Risk management includes establishing robust internal control systems, conducting risk assessments, and implementing mitigation strategies.

3.8 Ethical Conduct: Ethical conduct is an integral part of corporate governance. Companies should foster a culture of integrity, ethical behavior, and compliance with laws and regulations. Ethical conduct includes establishing a code of conduct, providing ethics training, and promoting a strong ethical tone at the top.

These principles serve as a framework for organizations to establish effective governance structures, build trust with stakeholders, and drive sustainable growth. Adhering to these principles helps companies maintain integrity, transparency, and accountability in their operations, leading to long-term value creation.

4. Key Elements of Corporate Governance

The key elements of corporate governance encompass various aspects that contribute to effective management, accountability, transparency, and the protection of stakeholder interests.

4.1 Board of Directors: The board of directors is a fundamental element of corporate governance. It comprises individuals responsible for overseeing the company's activities, setting strategic objectives, and monitoring management's performance. Key aspects related to the board of directors include:

4.1.1 Board Composition: The composition of the board plays a crucial role in effective governance. It includes a balance of executive directors (typically company executives) and independent directors who are not involved in the day-to-day operations of the company. Independent directors bring diverse expertise, experience, and perspectives to the board.

4.1.2 Board Independence: Independent directors are essential to ensure objective decision-making and safeguard the interests of minority shareholders. They bring unbiased judgment, challenge management, and contribute to the board's independence from the influence of the company's management.

4.1.3 Board Responsibilities: The board is responsible for setting the company's strategic direction, reviewing and approving significant policies, appointing and evaluating senior executives, and overseeing risk management practices. The board is also accountable for ensuring the company's compliance with laws, regulations, and ethical standards.

4.2 Shareholder Rights: Protecting and respecting shareholder rights is a crucial aspect of corporate governance. Shareholders have certain fundamental rights, including:

4.2.1 Voting Rights: Shareholders have the right to vote on key matters such as electing directors, approving significant corporate actions, and making changes to the company's articles of incorporation.

4.2.2 Information Rights: Shareholders have the right to receive timely and accurate information about the company's financial performance, operations, and governance practices. This includes access to financial reports, disclosures, and other relevant information.

4.2.3 Dividend Rights: Shareholders have the right to receive dividends, representing their share of the company's profits, as declared by the board of directors.

4.3 Transparency and Disclosure: Transparency and disclosure are critical for building trust and confidence among stakeholders. Key aspects related to transparency and disclosure include:

4.3.1 Financial Reporting: Companies must prepare and disclose financial statements, including balance sheets, income statements, and cash flow statements, in accordance with applicable accounting standards. Transparent financial reporting enables stakeholders to assess the company's financial health and performance accurately.

4.3.2 Non-Financial Reporting: In addition to financial reporting, companies are increasingly expected to disclose non-financial information related to environmental, social, and governance (ESG) factors. This includes disclosures on sustainability practices, social impact, diversity, and ethical considerations.

4.3.3 Related Party Transactions: Companies should disclose any transactions with related parties, such as directors, senior management, and their family members. Transparent disclosure helps mitigate conflicts of interest and ensures fair treatment of all stakeholders.

4.4 Risk Management: Effective risk management is vital for corporate governance. Companies should establish robust risk management frameworks and processes to identify, assess, and mitigate risks. Key aspects related to risk management include:

4.4.1 Risk Assessment: Companies should regularly assess potential risks that may affect their operations, financial performance, and reputation. This includes identifying operational, financial, legal, regulatory, and strategic risks.

4.4.2 Internal Controls: Companies should establish internal control systems to ensure that operations are conducted efficiently, assets are safeguarded, and financial reporting is accurate and reliable. Internal controls help mitigate risks and prevent fraudulent activities.

4.4.3 Audit Committees: Companies often have an audit committee consisting of independent directors responsible for overseeing the internal and external audit processes. The audit committee enhances the independence and effectiveness of internal and external audits, ensuring appropriate financial reporting and compliance with regulatory requirements.

4.5 Ethical Conduct and Corporate Culture: Promoting ethical conduct and fostering a strong corporate culture are essential for effective corporate governance. Companies should establish a culture of integrity, accountability, and ethical behavior. Key aspects related to ethical conduct and corporate culture include:

4.5.1 Code of Conduct and Ethics: Companies should develop and implement a code of conduct that outlines expected ethical standards for directors, executives, and employees. The code of conduct sets guidelines for appropriate behavior, conflict of interest management, and protection of whistleblowers.

4.5.2 Training and Awareness: Companies should provide regular training and awareness programs to educate directors, executives, and employees about ethical standards, compliance requirements, and the importance of responsible business conduct.

4.5.3 Tone at the Top: The board and senior management should set an example by demonstrating ethical behavior, integrity, and commitment to responsible governance practices. The "tone at the top" influences the corporate culture and the behavior of employees throughout the organization.

By focusing on these key elements, companies can establish a robust corporate governance framework that promotes accountability, transparency, and long-term value creation while safeguarding the interests of stakeholders.

5. Importance of Corporate Governance

The importance of corporate governance cannot be overstated as it plays a critical role in ensuring the integrity, transparency, and accountability of companies. Here are several key reasons why corporate governance is essential:

5.1 Protection of Shareholder Rights: Corporate governance safeguards the rights of shareholders, ensuring that their interests are protected and that they have a say in important decision-making processes. This includes the right to vote on key issues, access to accurate and timely information, and the ability to hold management accountable for their actions.

5.2 Prevention of Fraud and Mismanagement: Effective corporate governance mechanisms help detect and prevent fraudulent activities, mismanagement, and unethical practices within organizations. By establishing internal controls, risk management systems, and independent audit committees, corporate governance mitigates the risk of financial irregularities and enhances the reliability of financial reporting.

5.3 Enhancing Business Performance: Good corporate governance practices contribute to better business performance and sustainable growth. By promoting transparency and accountability, corporate governance encourages management to make informed decisions, align business strategies with long-term goals, and adopt responsible business practices. This, in turn, enhances the company's reputation, attracts investors, and builds trust among stakeholders.

5.4 Access to Capital and Lower Cost of Capital: Companies with strong corporate governance practices often find it easier to access capital from investors and financial institutions. Investors are more likely to invest in companies that demonstrate transparency, accountability, and good governance, as they perceive them to be less risky. Additionally, companies with effective corporate governance structures may enjoy a lower cost of capital due to increased investor confidence.

5.5 Protection of Stakeholder Interests: Corporate governance extends beyond shareholders and encompasses the interests of various stakeholders, including employees, customers, suppliers, and the wider community. By considering stakeholder interests, corporate governance fosters sustainable and responsible business practices, leading to long-term value creation and positive societal impact.

5.6 Regulatory Compliance: Strong corporate governance practices help companies comply with legal and regulatory requirements. By adhering to applicable laws and regulations, companies avoid legal disputes, penalties, and reputational damage. Compliance with corporate governance norms also provides assurance to regulators and helps maintain the overall stability and integrity of the business environment.

Thus, corporate governance is of paramount importance as it safeguards shareholder rights, prevents fraud, enhances business performance, attracts capital, protects stakeholder interests, and ensures compliance with laws and regulations. By promoting transparency, accountability, and responsible business practices, corporate governance contributes to the overall sustainability and success of organizations.

6. Evolving Trends in Corporate Governance

Corporate governance is a dynamic field that continuously evolves in response to changing business environments, emerging risks, technological advancements, and stakeholder expectations. Several evolving trends are shaping the landscape of corporate governance. Here are some key trends:

6.1 Focus on Sustainability and ESG: There is a growing emphasis on integrating environmental, social, and governance (ESG) factors into corporate governance practices. Stakeholders, including investors, customers, employees, and regulators, increasingly expect companies to demonstrate responsible business conduct and address sustainability challenges. Corporate governance frameworks are adapting to incorporate ESG considerations into decision-making processes, reporting, and accountability mechanisms.

6.2 Board Diversity and Inclusion: There is a growing recognition of the value of diverse perspectives and experiences in the boardroom. Organizations are placing greater importance on gender diversity, ethnic and cultural diversity, and diversity in skill sets and backgrounds. Efforts are being made to improve board diversity through voluntary targets, policies, and disclosure requirements to ensure more inclusive and representative governance bodies.

6.3 Stakeholder Engagement: There is a shift towards greater stakeholder engagement and dialogue. Companies are recognizing the importance of engaging with a wide range of stakeholders, including employees, customers, communities, and civil society organizations. This trend involves seeking input, considering stakeholder interests, and involving them in decision-making processes to ensure accountability and long-term value creation.

6.4 Technology and Digital Transformation: The rapid advancement of technology and digital transformation is influencing corporate governance practices. Boards need to understand and address the associated risks and opportunities, such as cybersecurity, data privacy, and artificial intelligence. Corporate governance frameworks are evolving to ensure effective oversight of technology-related issues, including digital ethics, data governance, and digital strategy alignment.

6.5 Executive Compensation and Incentives: There is increased scrutiny on executive compensation and a focus on aligning incentives with long-term sustainable performance. Stakeholders are demanding greater transparency and fairness in executive pay practices, and there are efforts to link compensation to environmental, social, and governance performance indicators. There is also an increased emphasis on clawback provisions and the use of performance-based pay to align executives' interests with long-term shareholder value.

6.6 Board Effectiveness and Evaluation: There is a growing emphasis on enhancing board effectiveness and conducting regular board evaluations. Boards are seeking to strengthen their governance practices by assessing their composition, skills, and processes. This trend includes evaluating individual director performance, board dynamics, and the overall effectiveness of the board in fulfilling its oversight responsibilities.

6.7 Shareholder Activism and Engagement: Shareholder activism is on the rise, with shareholders increasingly using their rights to influence governance practices and strategic decisions. Institutional investors are becoming more engaged in corporate governance, using their voting power and influence to push for improved governance standards and ESG practices. This trend is driving greater accountability and responsiveness to shareholder concerns.

6.8 Ethical Culture and Corporate Purpose: Companies are placing greater emphasis on ethical culture and corporate purpose as a foundation for effective governance. There is a focus on establishing strong ethical values, embedding them in organizational culture, and aligning corporate purpose with societal and stakeholder expectations. This trend involves promoting responsible business conduct, stakeholder value creation, and long-term sustainable growth.

These evolving trends highlight the need for organizations to adapt their governance frameworks to address emerging challenges and stakeholder expectations. By embracing these trends, companies can enhance transparency, accountability, and long-term value creation while fostering trust with stakeholders.

7. Summary
Chapter 1 serves as an introduction to the concept of corporate

governance, providing a comprehensive overview of its definition, importance, and key elements.

The chapter begins by defining corporate governance as a system of rules, practices, and processes that govern the way a company is directed, controlled, and managed. It emphasizes that corporate governance aims to ensure transparency, accountability, and fairness in a company's operations, while protecting the interests of shareholders and stakeholders. The chapter highlights the role of corporate governance in creating an environment of trust and confidence, attracting investors, and promoting sustainable business practices.

Next, the chapter explores the importance of corporate governance in detail. It explains that effective corporate governance is essential for preventing fraud, mismanagement, and unethical practices within companies. By establishing a clear set of rules and responsibilities, corporate governance helps to align the interests of shareholders and management, reducing agency conflicts. It also fosters long-term value creation, enhances the reputation of companies, and contributes to overall economic growth.

The chapter further examines the key elements of corporate governance. It discusses the role of the board of directors, highlighting their responsibilities in setting strategic objectives, overseeing management, and ensuring adherence to corporate governance principles. The chapter emphasizes the significance of shareholder rights and protection, including voting rights, access to information, and the ability to hold management accountable. It also underscores the importance of transparency and disclosure, ethical conduct, risk management, and stakeholder engagement within the framework of corporate governance.

Thus, Chapter 1 provides a comprehensive introduction to corporate governance, emphasizing its definition, importance, and key elements. It sets the foundation for understanding the role and significance of corporate governance in modern business environments.

References
1. Adams, R., Hermalin, B., & Weisbach, M. (2010). The Role of Boards of Directors in Corporate Governance: A Conceptual Framework and Survey. Journal of Economic Literature, 48(1), 58-107.
2. Aguilera, R., & Cuervo-Cazurra, A. (eds.). (2004). Corporate Governance in Global Capital Markets. Oxford University Press.
3. Bebchuk, L., & Roe, M. (2013). A Theory of Path Dependence in Corporate Ownership and Governance. Stanford Law Review, 52(1), 127-170.
4. Cadbury, A. (1992). Report of the Committee on the Financial Aspects of Corporate Governance. Gee Publishing.

5. Clarke, T. (2007). International Corporate Governance: A Comparative Approach. Routledge.

6. Coffee, J. (1991). The Rise of Dispersed Ownership: The Role of Law in the Separation of Ownership and Control. Yale Law Journal, 111(1), 1-82.

7. Dalton, D., Daily, C., Johnson, J., & Ellstrand, A. (1999). Number of Directors and Financial Performance: A Meta-Analysis. Academy of Management Journal, 42(6), 674-686.

8. Davis, G., Schoorman, F., & Donaldson, L. (1997). Toward a Stewardship Theory of Management. Academy of Management Review, 22(1), 20-47.

9. Financial Reporting Council. (2018). The UK Corporate Governance Code. Retrieved from https://www.frc.org.uk/getattachment/88bd8c45-50ea-4841-95b0-d2f4f48069a2/2018-UK-Corporate-Governance-Code-FINAL.pdf

10. Gillan, S., & Starks, L. (2003). Corporate Governance Proposals and Shareholder Activism: The Role of Institutional Investors. Journal of Financial Economics, 68(1), 137-167.

11. Hermalin, B., & Weisbach, M. (2012). Information Disclosure and Corporate Governance. Journal of Finance, 67(1), 195-233.

12. Jensen, M., & Meckling, W. (1976). Theory of the Firm: Managerial Behavior, Agency Costs, and Ownership Structure. Journal of Financial Economics, 3(4), 305-360.

13. La Porta, R., Lopez-de-Silanes, F., Shleifer, A., & Vishny, R. (1998). Law and Finance. Journal of Political Economy, 106(6), 1113-1155.

14. Mallin, C. (2016). Corporate Governance. Oxford University Press.

15. Monks, R., & Minow, N. (2018). Corporate Governance. John Wiley & Sons.

16. OECD. (2015). G20/OECD Principles of Corporate Governance. Retrieved from https://www.oecd.org/g20/topics/employment-and-social-policy/G20-OECD-PRINCIPLES-CORPORATE-GOVERNANCE.pdf

17. Pearce, J., & Zahra, S. (1991). The Relative Power of CEOs and Boards of Directors: Associations with Corporate Performance. Strategic Management Journal, 12(2), 135-153.

18. Pfeffer, J., & Salancik, G. (1978). The External Control of Organizations: A Resource Dependence Perspective. Harper & Row.

19. Shleifer, A., & Vishny, R. (1997). A Survey of Corporate Governance. Journal of Finance, 52(2), 737-783.

20. Solomon, J. (2010). Corporate Governance and Accountability. John Wiley & Sons.

21. The Cadbury Committee. (1992). Report of the Committee on the Financial Aspects of Corporate Governance: The Code of Best Practice. Gee Publishing.

22. Tricker, B. (2015). Corporate Governance: Principles, Policies, and Practices. Oxford University Press.

23. Turner, L. (1997). The Corporate Governance Debate: A Review of Current Research. Australian Accounting Review, 7(15), 4-10.

24. Useem, M. (1996). Investor Capitalism: How Money Managers are Changing the Face of Corporate America. Basic Books.

25. Yermack, D. (2017). Corporate Governance and Blockchains. Review of Finance, 21(1), 7-31.

CHAPTER 2
LEGAL AND REGULATORY FRAMEWORKS IN CORPORATE GOVERNANCE

Ms. Lovejit Kaur[2]

Chapter Abstract

In today's complex and interconnected business world, corporate governance plays a vital role in ensuring the accountability, transparency, and ethical conduct of corporations. To achieve effective corporate governance, robust legal and regulatory frameworks are necessary. This chapter will explore the key elements and principles of legal and regulatory frameworks in corporate governance, highlighting their significance in promoting responsible business practices.

1. The Role of Legal and Regulatory Frameworks

Legal and regulatory frameworks serve as the foundation for corporate governance by establishing rules, standards, and guidelines that companies must adhere to. These frameworks outline the rights, responsibilities, and obligations of various stakeholders, including shareholders, directors, executives, and employees. The primary objectives of legal and regulatory frameworks in corporate governance are:

a) Ensuring accountability and transparency: Legal frameworks require companies to disclose information on their financial performance, corporate structure, and decision-making processes. This promotes transparency and enables stakeholders to hold companies accountable for their actions.

b) Protecting stakeholders' interests: Regulatory frameworks aim to safeguard the interests of shareholders, employees, customers, and the wider

---

[2] Assistant Professor, School of Management Studies, CT University, Ludhiana

public. They establish mechanisms for protecting minority shareholders, preventing fraud and insider trading, and ensuring fair competition.

c) Promoting ethical conduct: Legal and regulatory frameworks set guidelines for ethical behavior and corporate social responsibility. They establish codes of conduct, anti-corruption measures, and environmental standards, fostering responsible business practices.

2. Legal and Regulatory Frameworks

2.1 Company Law and Corporate Governance

Company law is a fundamental component of the legal and regulatory framework in corporate governance. It provides the legal structure and framework within which companies operate, defining their rights, responsibilities, and obligations. This section will discuss the key aspects of company law that impact corporate governance.

2.1.1 Legal Form and Incorporation:

Company law establishes different legal forms of business entities, such as corporations, partnerships, and limited liability companies. The choice of legal form affects the governance structure and the rights and liabilities of shareholders, directors, and other stakeholders. For example, corporations typically have a separate legal personality, limited liability for shareholders, and a board of directors responsible for decision-making.

2.1.2 Shareholder Rights and Protections:

Company law sets out the rights and protections of shareholders, who are the owners of the company. These rights may include voting rights, dividend rights, preemptive rights, and the right to inspect company records. Shareholder protections aim to ensure fairness, transparency, and accountability in decision-making processes and protect minority shareholders from unfair treatment by controlling shareholders or management.

2.1.3 Directors' Duties and Responsibilities:

Company law outlines the duties and responsibilities of directors, who are entrusted with the management and supervision of the company. These duties typically include fiduciary duties (acting in the best interest of the company), duty of care (exercising due diligence and skill), duty of loyalty (avoiding conflicts of interest), and duty to act within their powers. Directors are also responsible for ensuring compliance with applicable laws and regulations and acting in the best interest of the company's stakeholders.

2.1.4 Board Structure and Composition:

Company law often prescribes the minimum and maximum number of directors, their qualifications, and the process for appointment, removal, and remuneration. It may also require the separation of key roles, such as the chairperson and CEO, and specify the composition of the board, including requirements for independent directors and diversity considerations. These provisions aim to enhance board independence, competence, and diversity, leading to better decision-making and oversight.

2.1.5 Financial Reporting and Disclosure:

Company law typically mandates financial reporting and disclosure requirements to ensure transparency and accountability. These requirements include preparing and publishing audited financial statements, annual reports, and interim financial statements. The law may also govern the disclosure of material information to shareholders, regulators, and the public, ensuring that stakeholders have access to relevant and accurate information for informed decision-making.

2.1.6 Shareholder Meetings and Voting:

Company law governs the procedures for shareholder meetings, including annual general meetings (AGMs) and extraordinary general meetings (EGMs). It establishes requirements for notice, quorum, voting, and proxy voting. Shareholders have the opportunity to exercise their voting rights on matters such as the election of directors, approval of financial statements, executive compensation, and major corporate transactions. The law ensures that shareholders can participate in corporate decision-making and hold management accountable.

2.1.7 Corporate Transactions and Mergers:

Company law provides regulations and procedures for significant corporate transactions, such as mergers, acquisitions, and takeovers. These regulations aim to protect the interests of shareholders and ensure fair treatment in such transactions. The law may require approvals from shareholders, independent evaluations, and disclosure of relevant information to ensure transparency and fairness.

2.1.8 Corporate Governance Codes and Compliance:

In addition to statutory requirements, company law may encourage or require companies to comply with corporate governance codes or guidelines. These codes provide best practice recommendations and principles for good governance, covering areas such as board composition, risk management, remuneration, and shareholder rights. Compliance with these codes may be voluntary or mandated by regulatory bodies, and companies are encouraged to adopt them to enhance their governance practices.

Thus, Company law plays a crucial role in shaping the legal and regulatory framework for corporate governance. It provides the legal structure for companies, defines the rights and responsibilities of stakeholders, and establishes mechanisms for accountability, transparency, and fairness. Understanding and complying with company law is essential for companies to operate ethically, protect shareholder interests, and foster trust among stakeholders.

2.2 Securities and Exchange Board of India (SEBI)

The Securities and Exchange Board of India (SEBI) is the regulatory authority responsible for overseeing and regulating the securities market in India. It plays a crucial role in establishing and enforcing the legal and regulatory framework for corporate governance in the country. This section will discuss the key functions and responsibilities of SEBI in promoting corporate governance.

2.2.1 Regulation and Oversight:

SEBI is empowered by the Securities and Exchange Board of India Act, 1992, to regulate and oversee various aspects of the securities market. It formulates rules, regulations, and guidelines to ensure fair and transparent practices in corporate governance. SEBI's regulatory authority extends to listed companies, stock exchanges, intermediaries, and other entities involved in the securities market.

2.2.2 Listing and Disclosure Requirements:

SEBI lays down listing requirements that companies must comply with to get listed on stock exchanges in India. These requirements include corporate governance provisions, such as the composition and independence of the board of directors, disclosure of financial information, related-party transactions, and timely disclosure of material events. SEBI's objective is to ensure that listed companies adhere to high standards of transparency, accountability, and investor protection.

2.2.3 Corporate Governance Codes and Guidelines:

SEBI has issued several corporate governance codes and guidelines to promote best practices in corporate governance among listed companies. The SEBI (Listing Obligations and Disclosure Requirements) Regulations, 2015, incorporates these codes and guidelines. They cover various aspects of corporate governance, including board composition, independent directors, committees of the board, executive compensation, related-party transactions, risk management, and shareholder rights. Compliance with these codes is mandatory for listed companies.

2.2.4 Insider Trading and Market Manipulation:

SEBI is responsible for regulating and preventing insider trading and market manipulation in the securities market. It has established stringent regulations and monitoring mechanisms to detect and deter these illegal activities. SEBI's objective is to ensure a level playing field for all market participants and protect the interests of investors.

2.2.5 Investor Protection and Education:

SEBI places significant emphasis on investor protection and education. It has established robust mechanisms for handling investor grievances and disputes, including the establishment of the Securities Appellate Tribunal. SEBI also conducts investor awareness programs and disseminates information and guidelines to educate investors about their rights, risks, and responsibilities. By empowering investors, SEBI aims to promote informed decision-making and strengthen investor confidence in the securities market.

2.2.6 Enforcement and Disciplinary Actions:

SEBI has the power to enforce compliance with its regulations and take disciplinary actions against entities that violate securities laws or engage in fraudulent or unfair practices. It can impose penalties, initiate legal proceedings, and suspend or cancel registrations of market intermediaries found guilty of misconduct. SEBI's enforcement actions serve as a deterrent and reinforce the importance of adherence to corporate governance norms.

2.2.7 Continuous Monitoring and Regulatory Updates:

SEBI maintains a vigilant approach through continuous monitoring of the securities market and evolving regulatory landscape. It regularly updates its regulations, guidelines, and codes to align with international best practices and address emerging challenges. SEBI keeps a close watch on market developments, corporate events, and changes in global regulatory frameworks to ensure that its regulatory framework remains robust and effective.

Thus, the Securities and Exchange Board of India (SEBI) plays a critical role in promoting corporate governance in the Indian securities market. Through its regulatory authority, oversight, and enforcement functions, SEBI establishes and enforces rules, regulations, and codes to ensure fair, transparent, and accountable practices in corporate governance. SEBI's efforts are aimed at safeguarding investor interests, enhancing market integrity, and fostering trust and confidence in the Indian securities market.

2.3 Role of Reserve Bank of India (RBI)

The Reserve Bank of India (RBI) is the central bank of India and plays a crucial role in the legal and regulatory framework for corporate governance. While its primary mandate is monetary policy and financial stability, the RBI also exercises regulatory and supervisory authority over banks and financial institutions. This section will discuss the key functions and responsibilities of the RBI in promoting corporate governance in India.

2.3.1 Banking Regulation and Supervision:

The RBI is responsible for regulating and supervising banks and financial institutions operating in India. It formulates and enforces prudential regulations, guidelines, and standards to ensure the soundness and stability of the banking system. These regulations encompass various aspects of corporate governance, including the composition and independence of boards, risk management practices, disclosure requirements, and internal controls. The RBI's oversight helps promote transparency, accountability, and risk management in the banking sector.

2.3.2 Corporate Governance Guidelines for Banks:

The RBI has issued comprehensive guidelines on corporate governance for banks. These guidelines set out principles and best practices that banks are expected to adhere to, covering areas such as board composition, appointment and remuneration of directors, risk management frameworks, internal controls, and disclosures. The guidelines aim to enhance governance standards in banks, strengthen risk management practices, and protect the interests of depositors and stakeholders.

2.3.3 Appointment and Fit and Proper Criteria:

The RBI plays a crucial role in the appointment of directors and top management personnel in banks. It sets "fit and proper" criteria for individuals holding key positions in banks, including directors and CEOs. The RBI assesses the integrity, competence, and track record of these individuals before granting approval for their appointments. This process ensures that banks are led by individuals with the necessary qualifications, expertise, and ethical standards to fulfill their fiduciary responsibilities.

2.3.4 Regulation of Related-Party Transactions:

The RBI regulates and monitors related-party transactions in banks to prevent conflicts of interest and protect the interests of depositors and stakeholders. It has set limits and guidelines for such transactions, ensuring transparency, fairness, and proper governance practices. The RBI's oversight helps mitigate the risks associated with related-party transactions and promotes good governance in banks.

2.3.5 Corporate Governance in Non-Banking Financial Companies (NBFCs):

In addition to banks, the RBI has regulatory oversight over Non-Banking Financial Companies (NBFCs). It issues guidelines and regulations that govern the corporate governance practices of NBFCs, ensuring compliance with prudential norms, risk management, and governance requirements. The RBI's supervision helps maintain the integrity and stability of the NBFC sector and protects the interests of investors and borrowers.

2.3.6 Enforcement and Disciplinary Actions:

The RBI has the authority to enforce compliance with its regulations and take disciplinary actions against banks and NBFCs that violate regulatory requirements or engage in fraudulent or unethical practices. It can impose penalties, initiate legal proceedings, and take corrective measures to address governance failures. The RBI's enforcement actions serve as a deterrent and promote accountability in the financial sector.

2.3.7 Promotion of Financial Inclusion and Investor Education:

The RBI plays a significant role in promoting financial inclusion and investor education. It formulates policies and initiatives aimed at extending banking services to underserved areas and populations. The RBI also conducts financial literacy programs and awareness campaigns to educate the public about financial products, risks, and rights. By promoting financial inclusion and investor education, the RBI contributes to a more inclusive and informed financial system.

Thus, the Reserve Bank of India (RBI) plays a vital role in promoting corporate governance in the Indian banking and financial sector. Through its regulatory and supervisory functions, the RBI establishes and enforces governance norms, guidelines, and standards for banks and NBFCs. The RBI's oversight helps ensure transparency, accountability, and stability in the financial system, protecting the interests of depositors, investors, and stakeholders. By promoting sound governance practices, the RBI contributes to the overall strength and resilience of India's financial sector.

2.4 Other Regulatory Bodies and Codes

In addition to the Securities and Exchange Board of India (SEBI) and the Reserve Bank of India (RBI), there are several other regulatory bodies and codes that contribute to the legal and regulatory framework for corporate governance in India. These bodies and codes play a significant role in ensuring compliance, transparency, and accountability in various sectors. This section will discuss some of the key regulatory bodies and codes relevant to corporate governance in India.

2.4.1 Ministry of Corporate Affairs (MCA):

The Ministry of Corporate Affairs (MCA) is the primary regulatory body responsible for the administration and enforcement of company law in India. It formulates and updates the Companies Act, which sets out the legal framework for the establishment, governance, and dissolution of companies. The MCA plays a critical role in ensuring compliance with company law provisions, promoting transparency, and protecting the interests of stakeholders.

2.4.2 National Financial Reporting Authority (NFRA):

The National Financial Reporting Authority (NFRA) is an independent regulatory body established under the Companies Act, 2013. NFRA is responsible for overseeing the quality of financial reporting and auditing practices of certain class of companies, including listed companies and large unlisted companies. NFRA's mandate includes monitoring compliance with accounting standards, conducting investigations into financial reporting misconduct, and imposing penalties for non-compliance.

2.4.3 Insurance Regulatory and Development Authority of India (IRDAI):

The Insurance Regulatory and Development Authority of India (IRDAI) is the regulatory body for the insurance sector in India. It establishes and enforces regulations and guidelines to ensure sound governance practices in insurance companies. IRDAI's regulatory framework covers areas such as corporate governance, risk management, solvency requirements, and disclosures. It aims to protect the interests of policyholders and promote stability and efficiency in the insurance sector.

2.4.4 Pension Fund Regulatory and Development Authority (PFRDA):

The Pension Fund Regulatory and Development Authority (PFRDA) regulates and oversees the pension sector in India. PFRDA formulates regulations and guidelines to ensure proper governance and protection of the interests of pension fund subscribers. It establishes governance standards for pension fund managers, custodians, and other entities in the pension industry. PFRDA's regulatory framework aims to promote transparency, accountability, and sustainability in the pension sector.

2.4.5 National Corporate Governance Committee (NCGC):

The National Corporate Governance Committee (NCGC) was constituted by SEBI in 2017 to suggest improvements in corporate governance practices in India. The NCGC has made recommendations on various aspects of corporate governance, including board composition, related-party transactions, risk management, and whistle-blower mechanisms. While the recommendations of NCGC are not legally binding, they serve as important guidance for companies and contribute to the development of corporate governance practices.

2.4.6 Institute of Company Secretaries of India (ICSI):

The Institute of Company Secretaries of India (ICSI) is a professional body responsible for promoting and regulating the profession of company secretaries in India. ICSI issues guidelines and codes of conduct for company secretaries, who play a critical role in ensuring compliance with corporate governance norms. The ICSI's guidelines emphasize the importance of ethical conduct, transparency, and good governance practices for company secretaries.

2.4.7 Corporate Governance Codes and Initiatives:

In addition to regulatory bodies, various industry bodies and associations have developed their own corporate governance codes and initiatives. For example, the Confederation of Indian Industry (CII) has developed a voluntary code of corporate governance, which sets out principles and practices for listed companies. Similarly, the Federation of Indian Chambers of Commerce and Industry (FICCI) has issued guidelines on corporate governance for its member companies. These codes provide additional guidance and best practices for companies to enhance their governance standards.

Thus, the legal and regulatory framework for corporate governance in India extends beyond SEBI and RBI. Regulatory bodies such as the Ministry of Corporate Affairs, NFRA, IRDAI, and PFRDA contribute to establishing and enforcing governance norms in their respective sectors. Additionally, industry bodies and professional associations play a role in developing codes and guidelines to promote good governance practices. These collective efforts aim to ensure compliance, transparency, and accountability in corporate governance, ultimately safeguarding the interests of stakeholders and fostering investor confidence.

3. Summary

In this chapter, we explored the legal and regulatory frameworks in corporate governance. We began by discussing the importance of company law in establishing the rights and responsibilities of stakeholders and ensuring accountability, transparency, and fairness. We then delved into the role of the Securities and Exchange Board of India (SEBI) in regulating and overseeing the securities market. SEBI's functions include formulating rules, listing requirements, and corporate governance codes to promote transparency and protect investor interests.

Next, we examined the role of the Reserve Bank of India (RBI) in the legal and regulatory framework. The RBI regulates and supervises banks and financial institutions, setting guidelines for corporate governance, related-party transactions, and appointment criteria. It contributes to the stability and soundness of the financial sector and protects the interests of depositors and stakeholders.

Finally, we explored other regulatory bodies and codes that play a role in corporate governance, such as the Ministry of Corporate Affairs, National Financial Reporting Authority, Insurance Regulatory and Development Authority of India, and Pension Fund Regulatory and Development Authority. These bodies establish regulations, guidelines, and codes to promote good governance practices in their respective sectors.

Overall, this chapter highlights the significance of the legal and regulatory framework in shaping corporate governance practices. Understanding and complying with these frameworks are essential for companies to operate ethically, protect shareholder interests, and foster trust among stakeholders.

References
1.   Adams, R. B., & Ferreira, D. (2009). Women in the boardroom and their impact on governance and performance. Journal of Financial Economics, 94(2), 291-309.
2.   Bebchuk, L. A., & Roe, M. J. (Eds.). (2013). The Oxford handbook of corporate law and governance. Oxford University Press.
3.   Black, B. S., & Carvalho, S. G. (2008). The legal environment of corporate governance. In Handbook of Corporate Finance: Empirical Corporate Finance (Vol. 2, pp. 479-583). Elsevier.
4.   Coffee, J. C., Jr. (2012). Corporate governance: Principles, policies, and practices. Oxford University Press.
5.   Dey, A., Engel, E., & Liu, X. (2011). CEO and board chair roles: To split or not to split? Journal of Corporate Finance, 17(5), 1595-1618.
6.   Gill, A., & Mathur, N. (Eds.). (2014). Corporate governance in India: Change and continuity. Routledge.
7.   Gompers, P., & Ishii, J. L. (2002). Corporate governance and equity

prices. The Quarterly Journal of Economics, 117(1), 107-155.

8.   Hermalin, B. E., & Weisbach, M. S. (2012). Understanding corporate governance through learning models of managerial competence. Journal of Economic Literature, 50(1), 72-115.

9.   Hillman, A. J., & Dalziel, T. (2003). Boards of directors and firm performance: Integrating agency and resource dependence perspectives. Academy of Management Review, 28(3), 383-396.

10.   Jensen, M. C. (1993). The modern industrial revolution, exit, and the failure of internal control systems. Journal of Finance, 48(3), 831-880.

11.   Khanna, T., & Palepu, K. (2000). Is group affiliation profitable in emerging markets? An analysis of diversified Indian business groups. Journal of Finance, 55(2), 867-891.

12.   La Porta, R., Lopez-de-Silanes, F., & Shleifer, A. (1999). Corporate ownership around the world. The Journal of Finance, 54(2), 471-517.

13.   Mahapatra, S., & Sethi, D. (2018). Corporate governance practices and firm performance: Evidence from Indian listed companies. Corporate Governance: The International Journal of Business in Society, 18(4), 693-711.

14.   Mallin, C. A. (2016). Corporate governance. Oxford University Press.

15.   Monks, R. A. G., & Minow, N. (2011). Corporate governance (5th ed.). John Wiley & Sons.

16.   Pucheta-Martínez, M. C., & Bel-Oms, I. (2020). Legal origin and corporate governance: A comprehensive review. Journal of Corporate Finance, 60, 101542.

17.   Shleifer, A., & Vishny, R. W. (1997). A survey of corporate governance. Journal of Finance, 52(2), 737-783.

18.   Tricker, B. (2015). Corporate governance: Principles, policies, and practices. Oxford University Press.

19.   Vafeas, N. (1999). Board meeting frequency and firm performance. Journal of Financial Economics, 53(1), 113-142.

20.   Yermack, D. (1996). Higher market valuation of companies with a small board of directors. Journal of Financial Economics, 40(2), 185-211.

CHAPTER 3
THE ROLE OF THE BOARD OF DIRECTORS IN CORPORATE GOVERNANCE
Dr. Kangan Sayal[3]

Chapter Summary

In corporate governance, the board of directors plays a critical role in overseeing the management and operations of a company. The board serves as the ultimate decision-making body, responsible for setting the strategic direction, monitoring performance, and ensuring accountability to shareholders and other stakeholders. This chapter provides an in-depth exploration of the board of directors' responsibilities, composition, structure, and best practices in corporate governance.

1. Who is a Director?

A director is an individual who serves on the board of directors of a company or organization. Directors are appointed or elected by shareholders or other stakeholders to provide oversight, make important decisions, and represent the interests of the company and its shareholders.

Directors have fiduciary duties to act in the best interests of the company, exercise due care and diligence, and avoid conflicts of interest. They are responsible for setting the strategic direction of the company, monitoring its performance, appointing and evaluating top executives, and ensuring compliance with laws and regulations.

The specific roles and responsibilities of directors may vary depending on the jurisdiction and the type of organization. In publicly traded companies,

[3] Assistant Professor, School of Management Studies, CT University, Ludhiana

directors are accountable to shareholders and are expected to act in their best interests. In nonprofit organizations, directors focus on advancing the organization's mission and serving the interests of the community or beneficiaries.

Directors often possess diverse backgrounds, skills, and expertise relevant to the organization's industry or sector. They may come from various professional fields such as finance, law, marketing, operations, or technology. The composition of the board of directors typically includes a mix of executive directors (such as the CEO) and non-executive directors (independent directors who are not part of the company's management team).

Overall, directors play a crucial role in corporate governance by providing strategic guidance, overseeing management, and ensuring accountability and transparency within the organization.

2. Types of Directors

There are different types of directors that can serve on a board, each with distinct roles and responsibilities. The specific types of directors may vary depending on the jurisdiction and the organization's governance structure. Here are some common types of directors:

• Executive Directors: Executive directors are individuals who hold executive positions within the organization. They are typically involved in the day-to-day management of the company and have specific operational responsibilities. Executive directors, such as the CEO, CFO, or COO, provide insight into the company's operations and implement strategic decisions made by the board.

• Non-Executive Directors: Non-executive directors (NEDs) are individuals who do not hold executive positions within the organization. They provide an independent perspective and oversight to the board. NEDs often have diverse backgrounds, expertise, and industry knowledge that contribute to the board's decision-making process. They typically bring broader external experience and may serve on multiple boards simultaneously.

• Independent Directors: Independent directors are a subset of non-executive directors who do not have any significant relationships with the company, its management, or its major shareholders. Independence is crucial to ensure objectivity and avoid conflicts of interest. Independent directors provide an unbiased viewpoint, challenge management when necessary, and enhance transparency and accountability.

• Inside Directors: Inside directors are individuals who are affiliated with the company in some way, either as executive directors or through their significant business relationships. They may have a deeper understanding of the company's operations, culture, and industry dynamics. Inside directors offer valuable insights and bridge the gap between the board and management.

- Outside Directors: Outside directors are independent directors who have no affiliation with the company beyond their board membership. They bring a fresh perspective and objectivity to the decision-making process. Outside directors are less likely to be influenced by internal dynamics and can critically assess the company's strategies, risks, and governance practices.
- Nominee Directors: Nominee directors are individuals appointed or nominated by specific shareholders or stakeholder groups, such as venture capitalists, institutional investors, or government entities. Nominee directors represent the interests of these specific groups and provide their insights and expertise to the board. However, they still have a fiduciary duty to act in the best interests of the company as a whole.
- Advisory Directors: Advisory directors, also known as directors emeritus or honorary directors, are individuals who are invited to serve on the board due to their extensive knowledge, experience, or industry reputation. While they may not have voting rights, advisory directors provide guidance and strategic advice based on their expertise and networks.

It's important to note that the composition of the board should be carefully considered to ensure a balance of skills, independence, diversity, and expertise. Different organizations may have specific requirements for the mix and number of these director types based on regulatory requirements, corporate governance guidelines, and the nature of the business.

3. Appointment of a director as per Section 152 of the Companies Act 2013

Section 152 of the Companies Act 2013 came into force on 1st April 2014. As far as the appointment is concerned, this Section deals with the following:

- Appointment of first directors; and
- appointment of directors at general meetings.

a) Appointment of First Directors:

- In the case of a newly incorporated company, the first directors are appointed at the time of incorporation.
- The subscribers to the company's memorandum, who are individuals, shall be deemed as the first directors of the company.
- The first directors can hold office until the directors are appointed in accordance with the provisions of the Act.

b) Appointment of Directors at General Meetings:

- Directors, other than the first directors, are appointed by shareholders at general meetings.
- The Act specifies that one-third of the total directors or the number nearest to one-third, excluding the first directors, must retire by rotation at every Annual General Meeting (AGM).

- The retiring directors may offer themselves for re-appointment.
- If a director does not offer himself/herself for re-appointment or if the shareholders do not reappoint a retiring director, the vacancy created by their retirement must be filled by electing a new director.
- The appointment of directors at general meetings is done by passing an ordinary resolution, except in certain cases where a special resolution may be required as per the Act.

4. Composition and Structure of the Board of Directors

The composition and structure of the board of directors play a crucial role in ensuring effective corporate governance. Here are some key considerations for the composition and structure of the board:

4.1 Independence: Having independent directors on the board is important for impartial decision-making. Independent directors are individuals who do not have any material or pecuniary relationships with the company or its management that could compromise their objectivity. They bring an external perspective, challenge management when necessary, and act as a safeguard against potential conflicts of interest. Many corporate governance codes and regulations require a minimum number or percentage of independent directors on the board.

4.2 Diversity: A diverse board brings a wide range of experiences, skills, perspectives, and backgrounds to the decision-making process. Diversity can encompass various dimensions, including gender, ethnicity, age, professional expertise, industry knowledge, and cultural backgrounds. Having a diverse board enhances the quality of discussions, improves problem-solving, and enables better representation of stakeholders' interests.

4.3 Skills and Expertise: The board should consist of directors who possess the skills, knowledge, and expertise relevant to the company's industry, operations, and strategic goals. This may include financial acumen, legal expertise, marketing insights, technology proficiency, risk management experience, international business knowledge, or specific industry knowledge. By having a mix of complementary skills, the board can effectively oversee and guide the company's activities.

4.4 Size: The size of the board is an important consideration. A board that is too large can hinder effective decision-making and communication, whereas a board that is too small may lack diverse perspectives. The optimal size of the board depends on various factors, including the company's size, complexity, industry, and governance requirements. Striking a balance is crucial to facilitate efficient discussions and collaborative decision-making.

4.5 Committees: Boards often establish committees to focus on specific areas of responsibility, such as audit, compensation, governance, and risk. Committee members should possess the necessary expertise and independence to fulfill their respective roles effectively. These committees assist the board in in-depth analysis, oversight, and decision-making within their respective domains. Committee composition should reflect the skills and knowledge required to address the specific issues at hand.

4.6 Tenure and Succession Planning: Regular refreshment and rotation of directors are essential for the board's vitality and continuity. Establishing tenure limits and implementing robust succession planning processes help ensure a continuous infusion of fresh perspectives, skills, and diversity. Succession planning involves identifying and developing potential candidates for director positions, considering the future needs of the organization, and planning for smooth transitions.

4.7 Board Evaluation: Regular board evaluations are important to assess the board's performance, effectiveness, and dynamics. The evaluation process can help identify areas for improvement, such as the board's composition, processes, and relationships with management. Self-evaluations, external evaluations, or a combination of both methods can be utilized to provide feedback and facilitate continuous improvement.

Thus, the composition and structure of the board should prioritize independence, diversity, relevant expertise, and effective governance practices. A well-structured board ensures robust decision-making, proper oversight, and accountability to stakeholders.

5. Roles and Responsibilities of Board of Directors

The board of directors plays a crucial role in corporate governance and is responsible for overseeing the management and strategic direction of a company. Their primary duties and responsibilities include:

5.1 Strategic Planning: The board is responsible for setting the company's overall strategic direction and ensuring that it aligns with the organization's mission and long-term objectives. They participate in the development and approval of strategic plans, including major business initiatives, mergers and acquisitions, and expansion into new markets.

5.2 Oversight of Management: The board appoints, evaluates, and provides guidance to the senior management team, including the CEO or managing director. They ensure that the company has competent leadership in place and that management's actions are consistent with the company's goals and values.

5.3 Risk Management: The board oversees the company's risk management practices and ensures that appropriate risk management processes are in place. They assess and monitor potential risks to the organization, including financial, operational, legal, and reputational risks, and work with management to develop strategies for risk mitigation.

5.4 Financial Oversight: The board has a responsibility to ensure the financial integrity and stability of the company. They review and approve financial statements, audit reports, and significant financial transactions. The board also establishes financial policies and internal controls to safeguard the company's assets and ensure compliance with applicable laws and regulations.

5.4 Corporate Governance: The board ensures that the company operates with integrity and adheres to high standards of corporate governance. They establish corporate governance policies and practices, including codes of conduct and ethics, to guide the behavior of directors, executives, and employees. The board also ensures compliance with legal and regulatory requirements and fosters a culture of transparency and accountability.

5.6 Shareholder Relations: The board represents the interests of shareholders and acts as a liaison between the company and its shareholders. They communicate with shareholders, address their concerns, and provide regular updates on the company's performance and major developments. The board also oversees the implementation of policies to protect shareholder rights and enhance shareholder value.

5.7 Board Composition and Succession Planning: The board is responsible for selecting and appointing new directors, including independent directors, based on their skills, expertise, and experience. They ensure that the board has a diverse composition that can provide effective oversight and contribute to the company's success. The board also develops and implements succession plans for key board and executive positions.

5.8 Board Meetings and Decision-making: The board holds regular meetings to discuss and make important decisions on matters that affect the company. They review management reports, approve budgets and major investments, and provide strategic guidance. The board also ensures that decisions are made in the best interest of the company and its stakeholders.

5.9 Stakeholder Engagement: The board considers the interests of various stakeholders, including employees, customers, suppliers, and the community. They engage with stakeholders, understand their concerns, and make decisions that balance the interests of different stakeholder groups.

5.10 Evaluation and Development: The board evaluates its own performance, as well as the performance of individual directors and board committees. They identify areas for improvement and implement measures to enhance board effectiveness. The board also supports director development and education to ensure that directors have the necessary skills and knowledge to fulfill their roles.

Thus, the board of directors has a wide range of responsibilities, including strategic planning, oversight of management, risk management, financial oversight, corporate governance, shareholder relations, board composition and succession planning, decision-making, stakeholder engagement, and evaluation and development. Through their collective expertise and guidance, the board plays a critical role in driving the success and sustainability of the company.

6. Board Committees and their Functions

Board committees play a crucial role in assisting the board of directors in fulfilling its responsibilities and enhancing corporate governance. Here are some common board committees and their functions:

6.1 Audit Committee:

• Function: The audit committee oversees financial reporting, internal controls, risk management, and the external audit process.

• Responsibilities:

☐ Reviewing financial statements, accounting policies, and significant financial reporting issues.

☐ Monitoring the effectiveness of internal control systems.

☐ Assessing the adequacy of risk management practices.

☐ Appointing and interacting with the external auditors.

☐ Reviewing the audit plan and ensuring the independence of auditors.

☐ Addressing whistleblower complaints related to accounting and financial reporting.

6.2 Compensation Committee:

• Function: The compensation committee is responsible for determining executive compensation and overseeing compensation-related matters.

• Responsibilities:

☐ Establishing compensation policies and frameworks for executives and board members.

☐ Reviewing and approving executive compensation packages, including salaries, bonuses, equity grants, and other benefits.

☐ Ensuring compensation practices align with the company's strategy, performance, and long-term goals.

☐ Assessing and approving incentive plans and performance-based compensation.

☐ Monitoring compliance with regulatory requirements related to compensation.

6.3 Governance/Nominating Committee:

• Function: The governance/nominating committee focuses on board composition, governance practices, and director nominations.

• Responsibilities:

☐ Identifying, evaluating, and recommending qualified individuals for board nominations.

☐ Assessing the composition and effectiveness of the board and its committees.

☐ Developing and reviewing governance policies, codes of conduct, and board charters.

☐ Facilitating board and director evaluations.

☐ Overseeing the company's corporate governance practices and compliance.

6.4 Risk Committee:

• Function: The risk committee is responsible for identifying, assessing, and managing enterprise risks.

• Responsibilities:

☐ Identifying and evaluating key strategic, operational, financial, and compliance risks.

☐ Developing and implementing risk management policies and procedures.

☐ Monitoring risk mitigation measures and control systems.

☐ Assessing the effectiveness of the company's risk management framework.

☐ Providing regular reports to the board on risk-related matters.

6.5 Compliance and Ethics Committee:

• Function: The compliance and ethics committee oversees the company's compliance with legal and regulatory requirements and promotes ethical conduct.

• Responsibilities:

☐ Developing and implementing compliance and ethics policies and programs.

☐ Ensuring compliance with laws, regulations, and industry standards.

☐ Monitoring and addressing potential conflicts of interest.

☐ Overseeing whistleblower programs and investigations.

☐ Promoting a culture of ethical behavior and integrity throughout the organization.

6.6 Strategic Committee:

• Function: The strategic committee focuses on long-term strategic planning, business development, and growth opportunities.

• Responsibilities:

☐ Assessing industry trends, competitive landscape, and market opportunities.

☐ Reviewing and approving the company's strategic plans and initiatives.

☐ Monitoring the progress and implementation of strategic objectives.

☐ Evaluating potential mergers, acquisitions, partnerships, or divestitures.

☐ Providing guidance and recommendations on major business decisions.

☐

7. Independent Directors

7.1 Who are Independent Directors

Independent directors are individuals who serve on the board of directors of a company without having any significant relationships or affiliations that could compromise their impartiality and objectivity. Their independence is essential to ensure that they can provide unbiased oversight and decision-making. Independent directors are not involved in the day-to-day operations of the company and are not employed by the company.

The specific criteria for determining independence may vary depending on legal and regulatory requirements, corporate governance codes, and the company's own policies. However, some common characteristics of independent directors include:

• No Material Relationships: Independent directors should not have any material or pecuniary relationships with the company, its management, or its major shareholders. This includes avoiding any financial or personal interests that could interfere with their ability to act independently and in the best interests of the company.

• Non-Executive Status: Independent directors typically do not hold executive positions within the company. They are not involved in the day-to-day management and operations, ensuring that they can provide an objective perspective and oversight.

• External Perspective: Independent directors bring external experience, expertise, and diverse viewpoints to the board. They may have backgrounds in different industries, professions, or sectors, providing valuable insights and challenging conventional thinking.

• Skills and Expertise: Independent directors often possess specific skills, knowledge, and expertise relevant to the company's industry or operations. They bring specialized insights and contribute their expertise to board discussions and decision-making processes.

• Limited Board Relationships: Independent directors should not have long-standing relationships or dependencies with other directors on the board that could compromise their independence. They should be able to exercise independent judgment and challenge the status quo when necessary.

• Independence Assessments: Many companies and regulatory bodies require periodic assessments to determine the independence of directors. These assessments may include evaluating any potential conflicts of interest, analyzing financial relationships, and assessing the overall independence of each director.

7.2 Number of Directorships and Alternate Directors

In India, the number of directorships an individual can hold simultaneously and the appointment of alternate directors are regulated by the Companies Act, 2013 and the rules issued thereunder. Here are some key provisions:

7.2.1 Number of Directorships:

• As per Section 165 of the Companies Act, 2013, an individual can serve as a director in a maximum of 20 companies at any given time.

• Out of these 20 directorships, the individual can serve as a director in a maximum of 10 public companies.

• The limit of 20 directorships includes both public and private companies, but does not include directorships in dormant companies, alternate directorships, or directorships in Section 8 (non-profit) companies.

• If an individual already holds directorships in the maximum number of companies allowed, they must resign from some directorships before accepting new appointments.

7.2.2 Alternate Directors:

• The Companies Act, 2013 allows the appointment of alternate directors under Section 161.

• An alternate director can be appointed by the board of directors if the original director is absent from India for a period of not less than three months or has any other valid reason for not being available.

• The appointment of an alternate director must be approved by the board and recorded in the minutes of the board meeting.

• The alternate director holds office during the absence of the original director and ceases to be an alternate director when the original director resumes their position or the period of absence comes to an end.

It is important for companies and directors in India to comply with these provisions to ensure effective governance and adherence to the law. The limits on directorships aim to prevent overboarding and ensure that directors can dedicate sufficient time and attention to their roles. The appointment of alternate directors allows for continuity in board representation when directors are temporarily unavailable.

7.3 Directors' Remuneration in India

Directors' remuneration in India is governed by the Companies Act, 2013 and the rules prescribed thereunder. Here are some key points regarding directors' remuneration in India:

7.3.1 Remuneration Approval:

• The remuneration payable to directors, including managing directors, whole-time directors, and independent directors, must be approved by the shareholders of the company.

• The approval is obtained through an ordinary resolution at a general meeting, and the details of the remuneration are disclosed in the company's financial statements.

7.3.2 Remuneration to Non-Executive Directors:

• Non-executive directors, including independent directors, are generally entitled to receive sitting fees for attending board meetings and committee meetings. The amount of sitting fees is determined by the board of directors within the limits prescribed by the Companies Act and rules.

• Apart from sitting fees, non-executive directors may also receive commission based on the profits of the company, subject to the approval of shareholders.

• Independent directors are not eligible for stock options or any performance-linked incentives.

7.3.3 Remuneration to Managing Directors and Whole-Time Directors:

• The remuneration payable to managing directors and whole-time directors consists of various components, including a fixed component, variable component, perquisites, allowances, and other benefits.

• The total remuneration payable to managing directors and whole-time directors, including sitting fees and commission, is subject to certain limits prescribed under the Companies Act. The limits are based on the company's profits, net worth, and the approval of shareholders.

• The appointment and remuneration of managing directors and whole-time directors require the approval of the board of directors, the nomination and remuneration committee, and the shareholders through an ordinary resolution.

7.3.4 Disclosures:

• Companies are required to disclose the remuneration paid to directors, including the breakup of components, in their financial statements.

• The details of remuneration, including the names of directors and key managerial personnel receiving remuneration above certain thresholds, are disclosed in the annual report of the company.

It is important for companies in India to comply with the provisions of the Companies Act and the rules regarding directors' remuneration to ensure transparency, accountability, and fair compensation practices. The remuneration must be approved by shareholders and disclosed in the company's financial statements and annual reports.

7.4 Role and Duties of Independent Director

he role and duties of independent directors are crucial in ensuring effective corporate governance and protecting the interests of all stakeholders. Here are some key aspects of the role and duties of independent directors:

7.4.1 Independence and Objectivity:

• Independent directors are expected to bring an objective and unbiased perspective to board discussions and decision-making processes.

• They should act in the best interests of the company and all its stakeholders, without being influenced by personal or external interests.

• Independence is vital to provide a check and balance on the actions of the management and promote transparency and accountability.

7.4.2 Oversight and Governance:

• Independent directors play a vital role in overseeing the performance of the company, its management, and its compliance with laws, regulations,

and ethical standards.
- They actively participate in board and committee meetings, providing their expertise and independent judgment on matters such as strategy, risk management, financial reporting, and internal controls.
- They contribute to the development and monitoring of corporate governance policies and practices, ensuring the company operates in a responsible and sustainable manner.

7.4.3 Decision-Making and Diligence:
- Independent directors contribute to informed decision-making by critically reviewing and analyzing proposals, strategies, financial statements, and other relevant information.
- They ask probing questions, challenge assumptions, and seek clarification to ensure that decisions are well-considered and in the best interests of the company.
- They exercise due diligence, staying updated on industry trends, regulatory changes, and emerging risks that may impact the company.

7.4.4 Stakeholder Protection:
- Independent directors act as representatives of minority shareholders and other stakeholders, safeguarding their interests and ensuring their voices are heard.
- They promote transparency, fairness, and accountability in dealings with shareholders, employees, customers, suppliers, and the broader community.
- They address conflicts of interest and potential related-party transactions, ensuring that such transactions are fair, transparent, and in the best interests of the company.

7.4.5 Committees and Special Assignments:
- Independent directors often serve on board committees, such as audit, remuneration, and nomination committees, bringing their expertise and independent judgment to these roles.
- They may be assigned specific responsibilities, such as leading investigations, overseeing risk management processes, or providing guidance on matters requiring specialized knowledge or experience.

7.4.6 Legal and Regulatory Compliance:
- Independent directors ensure that the company operates within the legal and regulatory framework and complies with applicable laws, regulations, and governance standards.
- They monitor the effectiveness of internal controls, risk management systems, and ethical practices to prevent fraud, misconduct, or non-compliance.

7.4.8 Continuous Learning and Development:
- Independent directors engage in ongoing learning and professional development to stay updated on governance practices, industry trends, and

emerging challenges.

- They participate in relevant training programs, workshops, and conferences to enhance their skills and knowledge.

The specific role and duties of independent directors may vary based on the company's size, industry, and regulatory requirements. However, their overarching responsibility is to act in the best interests of the company, shareholders, and other stakeholders, providing independent oversight, guidance, and support to promote effective corporate governance and sustainable long-term growth.

8. Disqualification of Directors

Disqualification of directors refers to the circumstances under which an individual is prohibited from serving as a director of a company. In India, the disqualification of directors is governed by the provisions of the Companies Act, 2013. Here are some key reasons for disqualification:

8.1 Non-Compliance and Default:

- Directors can be disqualified if they fail to comply with their statutory obligations under the Companies Act, such as filing annual returns, financial statements, or other required documents within the prescribed time.
- Non-payment of statutory fees, penalties, or any other amounts due to the company or regulatory authorities can also lead to disqualification.

8.2 Insolvency and Bankruptcy:

- Directors who are declared insolvent or have been adjudged as bankrupt by a competent court are disqualified from serving as directors.

8.3 Conviction of Offences:

- Directors convicted of certain offenses, including fraud, dishonesty, bribery, money laundering, or any offense involving moral turpitude, may be disqualified.
- Additionally, directors convicted of offenses related to the promotion, formation, or management of a company may face disqualification.

8.4 Contravention of Law:

- Directors who are found to have contravened provisions of the Companies Act, such as acting beyond their powers or using company resources for personal gain, may be disqualified.

8.5 Prohibited Activities:

- Directors engaged in activities prohibited by law, such as being a director of more than the maximum number of companies allowed or serving as a director while disqualified, can face disqualification.

8.6 Removal by Shareholders:

- Shareholders can remove a director by passing a special resolution in a general meeting, and the disqualified director cannot be reappointed for a specified period as per the Companies Act.

8.7 Regulatory Authority Disqualification:
• Certain regulatory authorities, such as the Securities and Exchange Board of India (SEBI) or the Reserve Bank of India (RBI), can disqualify individuals from serving as directors in specific circumstances within their regulatory domain.

It's important for directors to be aware of their responsibilities and obligations under the Companies Act and other relevant laws. Failure to fulfill these obligations can lead to disqualification, resulting in legal consequences and restrictions on serving as directors in other companies. Regular compliance, adherence to ethical standards, and timely filing of required documents are essential to avoid disqualification and maintain good standing as a director.

9. Vacation of office by the Directors

Vacation of office by directors refers to the circumstances under which a director's position becomes vacant or terminated. The Companies Act, 2013 in India specifies certain grounds for vacation of office. Let's explore some of these grounds:

9.1 Resignation: A director may voluntarily resign from their position by submitting a written resignation to the company. The resignation takes effect from the date it is received or from a specified future date, if any.

9.2 Expiry of Term: If a director's appointment is for a fixed term, their office will be vacated upon the expiry of that term unless they are reappointed or their appointment is renewed.

9.3 Removal by Shareholders: Shareholders have the power to remove a director from office by passing a special resolution at a general meeting. The Companies Act, 2013 lays down the procedure and requirements for the removal of directors.

9.4 Disqualification: Directors can be disqualified from holding office due to various reasons, as discussed earlier. If a director becomes disqualified as per the provisions of the Companies Act, their office will be vacated.

9.5 Bankruptcy or Insolvency: If a director is declared bankrupt or insolvent by a court, their office will be vacated. Bankruptcy or insolvency disqualifies an individual from serving as a director.

9.6 Death or Incapacity: The office of a director is automatically vacated upon their death or if they become incapacitated and unable to perform their duties.

9.7 Absence from Board Meetings: The Companies Act, 2013 states that if a director fails to attend board meetings for a continuous period of one year without obtaining leave of absence from the board, their office may be vacated. This provision emphasizes the importance of active participation and attendance at board meetings.

10. Best Governance Planning: Board Evaluation and Succession Planning

10.1 Board Evaluation:

Board evaluation is a critical process that assesses the performance, effectiveness, and dynamics of the board of directors. It helps identify areas of improvement and enhances the board's overall effectiveness. Here are key aspects of board evaluation:

• Objective Assessment: The evaluation should be conducted objectively, either internally or with the assistance of an external evaluator. The evaluation process should be confidential and allow for honest feedback from all board members.

• Comprehensive Evaluation Criteria: The evaluation criteria should cover various aspects, including board composition, individual director performance, board processes and procedures, strategic oversight, risk management, and board dynamics. It should align with the company's objectives and governance principles.

• Regular Evaluation Cycle: Board evaluations should be conducted periodically, typically annually, to ensure continuous improvement. Some companies may opt for a more frequent evaluation cycle, especially during times of significant change or challenges.

• Evaluation Methods: There are several methods to conduct board evaluations, such as surveys, questionnaires, interviews, or facilitated discussions. The chosen method should be appropriate for the organization's size, structure, and culture.

• Actionable Recommendations: The evaluation process should result in actionable recommendations for improvement. The board should prioritize and implement these recommendations to enhance its effectiveness and governance practices.

10.2 Succession Planning:

Succession planning involves identifying and developing future directors and executives to ensure a smooth transition when vacancies arise. It helps maintain continuity, build leadership capacity, and mitigate risks associated with leadership changes. Here are key considerations for effective succession planning:

• Robust Talent Identification: The board should identify potential candidates internally and externally who possess the skills, experience, and diversity required to fulfill future leadership roles. This includes considering candidates from different backgrounds and perspectives to enhance board effectiveness.

• Leadership Development Programs: The organization should implement leadership development programs that provide training, mentoring, and exposure to key areas of the business. These programs help groom potential successors and ensure a pipeline of capable leaders.

• Board Involvement: Succession planning should be a collaborative effort involving the board, CEO, and senior management. The board should actively participate in the identification and development of potential successors, ensuring alignment with the organization's strategic goals.

• Contingency Planning: Succession planning should include contingency plans for unexpected vacancies, such as sudden departures or emergencies. It ensures the organization can quickly fill critical positions with qualified individuals, minimizing disruptions to operations.

• Regular Review: Succession plans should be regularly reviewed and updated to reflect changing business needs, market conditions, and evolving leadership requirements. This helps the board adapt and respond effectively to future leadership challenges.

Both board evaluation and succession planning are crucial components of strong corporate governance. Regularly assessing board performance and preparing for leadership transitions contribute to the long-term success and sustainability of the organization.

11. Summary

This chapter provided a comprehensive overview of the board of directors in corporate governance, focusing on key aspects such as composition, structure, roles and responsibilities, board committees, independent directors, and board evaluation and succession planning.

The chapter explored the composition and structure of the board of directors. It emphasized the importance of having a diverse board with a mix of skills, expertise, and backgrounds. The chapter discussed the roles of various stakeholders in board composition, including shareholders, management, and regulatory requirements. Additionally, it highlighted the significance of board independence and the role of non-executive directors in providing objective oversight and governance.

Then chapter delved into the roles and responsibilities of the board of directors. It emphasized the board's key duties, such as setting strategic direction, monitoring performance, approving major decisions, and ensuring compliance with legal and ethical standards. The chapter also highlighted the importance of effective communication between the board and management, as well as the need for active engagement and informed decision-making.

The chapter then focused on board committees and their functions. It explained the purpose and responsibilities of various board committees, such as audit committees, compensation committees, and nomination committees. The chapter emphasized the significance of committee independence, expertise, and proper reporting mechanisms to ensure effective governance. Furthermore, it discussed the role of board committees in enhancing transparency, risk management, and financial oversight.

Lastly, the chapter addressed the role of independent directors and the importance of their presence on the board. It highlighted the value of independent directors in providing objective judgment, safeguarding the interests of minority shareholders, and ensuring proper corporate governance practices. The chapter also discussed the significance of board evaluation and succession planning in maintaining board effectiveness and leadership continuity.

Overall, this chapter provided a comprehensive understanding of the composition, structure, roles, and responsibilities of the board of directors, as well as the importance of board committees, independent directors, and board evaluation and succession planning in effective corporate governance.

References

1.   Adams, R. B., & Ferreira, D. (2009). Women in the boardroom and their impact on governance and performance. Journal of Financial Economics, 94(2), 291-309.

2.   Aggarwal, R. K., & Kyaw, N. A. (2019). Corporate boards, independent directors, and firm performance: A review and research agenda. International Journal of Management Reviews, 21(4), 461-483.

3.   Anderson, R. C., & Reeb, D. M. (2003). Founding-family ownership and firm performance: Evidence from the S&P 500. Journal of Finance, 58(3), 1301-1327.

4.   Beasley, M. S., Carcello, J. V., & Hermanson, D. R. (2016). Fraudulent financial reporting: 1987–2007. An analysis of US public companies. Contemporary Accounting Research, 33(2), 412-448.

5.   Byrd, J. W., & Hickman, K. A. (1992). Do outside directors monitor managers? Evidence from tender offer bids. Journal of Financial Economics, 32(2), 195-221.

6.   Daily, C. M., Dalton, D. R., & Cannella Jr, A. A. (2003). Corporate governance: Decades of dialogue and data. Academy of Management Review, 28(3), 371-382.

7.   Fama, E. F., & Jensen, M. C. (1983). Separation of ownership and control. The Journal of Law and Economics, 26(2), 301-325.

8.   Filatotchev, I., Jackson, G., & Nakajima, C. (2013). Corporate governance and national institutions: A review and emerging research agenda. Asia Pacific Journal of Management, 30(4), 965-986.

9.   Gompers, P. A., Ishii, J. L., & Metrick, A. (2003). Corporate governance and equity prices. The Quarterly Journal of Economics, 118(1), 107-155.

10.   Hermalin, B. E., & Weisbach, M. S. (2003). Boards of directors as an endogenously determined institution: A survey of the economic literature. Economic Policy Review, 9(1), 7-26.

11.   Jensen, M. C. (1993). The modern industrial revolution, exit, and the

failure of internal control systems. The Journal of Finance, 48(3), 831-880.

12. Johnson, S., Boone, P., Breach, A., & Friedman, E. (2000). Corporate governance in the Asian financial crisis. Journal of Financial Economics, 58(1-2), 141-186.

13. Judge, W. Q., & Zeithaml, C. P. (1992). Institutional and strategic choice perspectives on board involvement in the strategic decision process. Academy of Management Journal, 35(4), 766-794.

14. Kiel, G. C., & Nicholson, G. J. (2003). Board composition and corporate performance: How the Australian experience informs contrasting theories of corporate governance. Corporate Governance: An International Review, 11(3), 189-205.

15. Kosnik, R. D. (1987). Greenmail: A study of board performance in corporate governance. Administrative Science Quarterly, 32(2), 163-185.

16. Lorsch, J. W. (2009). Picking boards that perform. Harvard Business Review, 87(11), 92-100.

17. Millstein, I. M. (1998). Corporate governance: Improving board performance and accountability. Columbia Law Review, 98(3), 778-860.

18. Pfeffer, J., & Salancik, G. R. (2003). The external control of organizations: A resource dependence perspective. Stanford University Press.

19. Rajan, R. G., & Zingales, L. (1998). Which capitalism? Lessons from the East Asian crisis. Journal of Applied Corporate Finance, 11(3), 40-48.

20. Rosenstein, S., & Wyatt, J. G. (1990). Outside directors, board independence, and shareholder wealth. Journal of Financial Economics, 26(2), 175-191.

21. Shleifer, A., & Vishny, R. W. (1997). A survey of corporate governance. The Journal of Finance, 52(2), 737-783.

22. Singh, H., & Davidson III, W. N. (2003). Agency costs, ownership structure and corporate governance mechanisms. Journal of Banking & Finance, 27(5), 793-816.

23. Tirole, J. (2001). Corporate governance. Econometrica, 69(1), 1-35.

24. Uzzi, B. (1999). Embeddedness in the making of financial capital: How social relations and networks benefit firms seeking financing. American Sociological Review, 64(4), 481-505.

25. Yermack, D. (1996). Higher market valuation of companies with a small board of directors. Journal of Financial Economics, 40(2), 185-211.

CHAPTER 4
SHAREHOLDERS AND SHAREHOLDER RIGHTS
Dr. Kawal Nian Singh[4]

Chapter Abstract

Shareholders play a crucial role in corporate governance and have certain rights and responsibilities within a company. This chapter explores the concept of shareholders, their rights, and the importance of shareholder engagement in the corporate decision-making process. It also examines the legal frameworks and mechanisms that protect shareholder rights and promote transparency and accountability.

1. Understanding Shareholders

1.1 Definition of Shareholders

Shareholders are individuals, entities, or institutions that own shares or stock in a company. They are the legal owners of a portion of the company's equity and have a financial interest in its performance and success. Shareholders are recorded on the company's shareholder registry and hold shares that represent their ownership stake. Shareholders can range from individual investors to institutional investors such as mutual funds, pension funds, and other investment firms. Their ownership gives them certain rights, including the right to vote on significant corporate matters, such as the election of directors and approval of major decisions. Shareholders may also be entitled to receive dividends, which are distributions of the company's profits, and they may benefit from capital appreciation if the value of their shares increases. Shareholders' rights and obligations are typically governed by company laws, corporate governance guidelines, and the company's

---

[4] Associate Professor, School of Management Studies, CT University, Ludhiana

bylaws or articles of incorporation.

1.2 Types of Shareholders

Shareholders can be classified into various types based on their characteristics, motivations, and roles within a company. Some common types of shareholders include:

1.   Individual Shareholders: These are individual investors who purchase shares in a company with their personal funds. They may own shares for various reasons, such as seeking capital appreciation, receiving dividends, or participating in the company's growth.

2.   Institutional Shareholders: Institutional shareholders are large organizations or entities that invest on behalf of others. Examples include mutual funds, pension funds, insurance companies, and hedge funds. Institutional shareholders often hold significant stakes in companies and can have a substantial influence on corporate decisions.

3.   Founders and Management Shareholders: Founders are individuals who establish the company and often hold significant ownership stakes. Management shareholders are executives and key employees who may receive shares or stock options as part of their compensation packages.

4.   Strategic Shareholders: These shareholders acquire shares in a company with the intention of gaining strategic benefits, such as access to technology, markets, or synergies with their own businesses. Strategic shareholders may also seek to influence the company's operations or direction.

5.   Passive Shareholders: Passive shareholders are investors who hold shares without actively participating in the company's decision-making process. They are mainly interested in capital appreciation and dividends rather than playing an active role in governance.

6.   Activist Shareholders: Activist shareholders are individuals or groups who take an active role in influencing the company's policies, management, or strategic decisions. They may propose shareholder resolutions, engage in proxy battles, or advocate for specific changes within the company.

7.   Public Shareholders: Public shareholders are individuals or entities that own shares in publicly traded companies, whose shares are listed on stock exchanges and are available for trading to the general public.

8.   Private Shareholders: Private shareholders hold shares in privately held companies, which are not publicly traded on stock exchanges. These shares are typically held by a limited number of individuals or entities.

9.   Majority Shareholders: Majority shareholders are individuals or entities that hold a significant percentage of a company's shares, giving them substantial control and influence over corporate decisions.

10.   Minority Shareholders: Minority shareholders own a smaller

percentage of a company's shares, and their influence on decision-making is limited compared to majority shareholders.

Each type of shareholder brings its own perspectives, interests, and objectives to the table, shaping the dynamics of corporate governance and influencing the company's overall performance.

2. Shareholder Ownership and Voting Power

Ownership and voting power are fundamental aspects of shareholder rights and play a crucial role in corporate governance. In this section, we will discuss shareholder ownership, the significance of ownership stakes, and how voting power is exercised within a company.

2.1 Shareholder Ownership

Shareholder ownership refers to the proportionate ownership interest that shareholders hold in a company. This ownership is determined by the number of shares or stocks owned by the shareholder. When shareholders purchase shares, they acquire a portion of the company's equity, representing their ownership stake.

a. Equity Ownership: Shareholders are considered the legal owners of the company's equity. The equity represents the residual interest in the company's assets after deducting liabilities. Shareholders' ownership stakes determine their entitlement to the company's profits, assets, and dividends.

b. Types of Shares: Companies may issue different types of shares, such as common shares and preferred shares. Common shares represent basic ownership rights, including voting rights and a share in the company's profits. Preferred shares, on the other hand, typically have specific rights and preferences, such as priority in dividend payments or liquidation preferences.

c. Share Certificates and Electronic Ownership: Traditionally, shareholders were issued physical share certificates as evidence of their ownership. However, with the advent of electronic trading and dematerialization of shares, many jurisdictions now use electronic records to represent share ownership.

2.2 Significance of Ownership Stakes

The ownership stake held by shareholders carries significant implications for their rights and influence within a company. Here are a few key aspects:

a. Control and Decision-Making: Shareholders with larger ownership stakes generally have more control and influence over the company's decision-making process. They can exercise their voting power to elect directors, approve major decisions, and shape the company's strategic direction.

b. Economic Interests: Shareholders' ownership stakes directly impact their economic interests in the company. The value of their shares may appreciate or depreciate based on the company's performance, affecting their potential returns on investment. Shareholders may also receive dividends based on their ownership stakes.

c. Dilution and Preemptive Rights: In cases where companies issue new shares, existing shareholders may face dilution of their ownership stakes. However, preemptive rights may enable shareholders to maintain their proportional ownership by purchasing additional shares before they are offered to the public or other investors.

2.3 Voting Power

Voting power is a crucial element of shareholder rights, allowing shareholders to participate in important decision-making processes. Each share typically carries one vote, but the voting power can vary based on share classes or special rights attached to specific shares.

a. General Meetings: Shareholders exercise their voting power at general meetings, such as annual general meetings (AGMs) or extraordinary general meetings (EGMs). During these meetings, shareholders vote on various matters, including the election of directors, approval of financial statements, mergers, acquisitions, amendments to bylaws, and other significant corporate decisions.

b. Proxies and Proxy Voting: Shareholders who are unable to attend general meetings can appoint proxies to vote on their behalf. Proxies can be individuals or entities authorized to represent shareholders' interests and cast votes as per their instructions.

c. Majority Voting and Minority Rights: In most cases, decisions are made based on majority voting, where the outcome depends on the majority of votes cast. However, certain jurisdictions or corporate structures may provide protection for minority shareholders by requiring special majority or supermajority votes for specific decisions that may affect their rights or interests.

d. Voting Agreements and Coalitions: Shareholders may enter into voting agreements or form coalitions to collectively vote their shares in a coordinated manner. This can enhance their influence and help shape outcomes in line with their shared objectives.

e. Proxy Advisory Firms: Proxy advisory firms provide research and recommendations on shareholder proposals and voting matters. Institutional investors often rely on these firms' expertise to guide their voting decisions.

Effective voting power ensures that shareholders can participate in the governance of the company, safeguard their interests, and hold management accountable. It promotes transparency, accountability, and democratic decision-making within corporate structures.

3. Shareholder Activism

Shareholder activism refers to the actions taken by shareholders to actively engage with a company and influence its policies, practices, or strategic direction. Activist shareholders seek to drive change and enhance shareholder value by leveraging their ownership rights and advocating for specific reforms or improvements within the company. Shareholder activism can take various forms and is driven by different motivations, including financial gain, corporate governance concerns, social responsibility, or environmental sustainability.

Here are some key aspects of shareholder activism:

3.1 Objectives of Shareholder Activism: Shareholder activists pursue a range of objectives, including:

a. Governance Reforms: Activists may focus on improving corporate governance practices, such as board diversity, executive compensation, or shareholder rights.

b. Strategic Changes: Activists may push for strategic shifts, such as mergers, acquisitions, divestitures, or changes in the company's business model.

c. Environmental, Social, and Governance (ESG) Issues: Activists may advocate for companies to adopt responsible and sustainable practices, address environmental concerns, or promote social initiatives.

d. Financial Performance: Some activists aim to enhance shareholder value by targeting underperforming companies and proposing operational or structural changes to boost profitability.

3.2 Tactics and Strategies of Shareholder Activism: Shareholder activists employ various tactics to influence companies, including:

a. Proxy Contests: Activists may nominate their own candidates for the board of directors, challenging the incumbent directors and seeking shareholder support through proxy voting.

b. Shareholder Resolutions: Activists can propose resolutions on specific issues to be voted on at shareholder meetings. These resolutions can address governance matters, executive compensation, sustainability, or other concerns.

c. Engaging with Management and Boards: Activists may engage in direct discussions with company management or board members to express their concerns, propose changes, or seek resolutions.

d. Public Campaigns: Activists often utilize media and public relations campaigns to raise awareness, gain support, and apply pressure on companies to respond to their demands.

e. Litigation: In some cases, activists may resort to legal action, such as filing lawsuits or class-action suits, if they believe their rights as shareholders have been violated.

3.3 Activist Shareholders: Activist shareholders can include institutional investors, hedge funds, pension funds, or individual shareholders. They may have substantial ownership stakes or form alliances with other shareholders to amplify their influence.

a. Institutional Investors: Large institutional investors, such as pension funds and mutual funds, may engage in activism to protect the interests of their beneficiaries or investors and promote responsible investment practices.

b. Hedge Funds: Activist hedge funds often take significant positions in targeted companies and actively advocate for changes to unlock shareholder value.

c. Individual Investors: Individual shareholders can also engage in activism by submitting proposals, attending shareholder meetings, or joining forces with other like-minded shareholders.

3.4 Impact and Controversies: Shareholder activism has both supporters and critics. Proponents argue that it promotes better corporate governance, enhances accountability, and helps align companies with shareholder interests. Activists often point out corporate inefficiencies, champion stakeholder interests, and bring attention to ESG concerns. However, critics argue that some activists prioritize short-term gains over long-term sustainability or disrupt the stability and strategic vision of companies.

3.5 Regulatory Environment: The regulatory framework governing shareholder activism varies across jurisdictions. Regulations may address disclosure requirements, proxy voting rules, shareholder proposal thresholds, or measures to protect minority shareholders. Regulators strive to strike a balance between shareholder rights and the interests of all stakeholders.

Overall, shareholder activism serves as a mechanism to hold companies accountable and drive positive change. By leveraging their ownership rights and engaging in active dialogue, activist shareholders can contribute to more responsible, sustainable, and value-enhancing corporate practices.

4. Shareholders Responsibility

Shareholders have various responsibilities as owners of a company. While the specific responsibilities may vary depending on jurisdiction, corporate structure, and shareholder agreements, there are some common fundamental responsibilities that shareholders are expected to fulfill. Here are the key responsibilities of shareholders:

4.1 Exercising Voting Rights: Shareholders have the right to vote on significant corporate matters. It is their responsibility to actively participate in voting, especially during general meetings, to elect directors, approve financial statements, and make important decisions that impact the company's direction. Shareholders should make informed decisions based on their understanding of the issues at hand and their assessment of the company's best interests.

4.2 Monitoring Management: Shareholders have a responsibility to monitor the company's management. This involves staying informed about the company's performance, financial health, and strategic initiatives. Shareholders should critically evaluate management decisions, executive compensation, and corporate governance practices to ensure they align with shareholder interests and promote long-term value creation.

4.3 Protecting Shareholder Rights: Shareholders are responsible for protecting their own rights and the rights of other shareholders. This includes advocating for transparent and fair corporate practices, ensuring compliance with applicable laws and regulations, and preventing any actions that may undermine shareholder interests or dilute their ownership.

4.4 Engaging in Shareholder Activism: Shareholders have the option to engage in shareholder activism when they believe it is necessary to drive positive change within the company. Activism can involve advocating for improvements in governance, sustainability, social responsibility, or other areas of concern. Shareholders should exercise their activism rights responsibly, aiming to enhance long-term shareholder value and promote the company's overall well-being.

4.5 Exercising Ownership Duties: Shareholders have certain ownership duties that include acting in good faith, exercising due care, and acting in the best interests of the company and its shareholders as a whole. They should not use their ownership rights to pursue personal gain or engage in actions that could harm the company or other stakeholders.

4.6 Supporting Long-Term Value Creation: Shareholders have a responsibility to support the company's long-term value creation and sustainability. This involves taking a strategic perspective and considering the company's long-term prospects rather than focusing solely on short-term gains. Shareholders should encourage responsible management practices, consider environmental and social factors, and support the company's efforts to achieve sustainable growth.

4.7 Complying with Legal and Regulatory Obligations: Shareholders have a responsibility to comply with all applicable laws, regulations, and corporate governance guidelines. They should fulfill their obligations regarding the disclosure of their ownership interests, insider trading restrictions, and other legal requirements governing their involvement in the company.

4.8 Seeking Information and Transparency: Shareholders have a responsibility to seek relevant information about the company's operations, financial performance, and risk factors. They should actively participate in shareholder meetings, ask questions, and seek clarification on matters of concern. Shareholders should promote transparency and encourage the company to provide timely and accurate information to all shareholders.

4.9 Respecting Minority Shareholder Rights: Shareholders should respect the rights of minority shareholders and ensure their fair treatment. This includes considering their interests in decision-making processes, avoiding actions that unfairly disadvantage them, and advocating for appropriate minority shareholder protections.

4.10 Seeking Professional Advice: Shareholders may seek professional advice, such as legal, financial, or governance expertise, to fulfil their responsibilities effectively. This can help shareholders make informed decisions, understand their rights and obligations, and navigate complex corporate matters.

It is important to note that shareholders' responsibilities should be exercised in alignment with applicable laws, company bylaws, and shareholder agreements. Shareholders should also consider the company's specific circumstances, industry norms, and the interests of other stakeholders, such as employees, customers, and the broader community, while fulfilling their responsibilities as owners

5. Rights of the Shareholders

5.1 Economic Rights:

a. Dividend Rights: Shareholders have the right to receive a portion of the company's profits as dividends. Dividends are typically distributed in proportion to the number of shares owned by each shareholder. Dividend rights allow shareholders to share in the company's financial success and receive a return on their investment.

b. Preemptive Rights: Shareholders have the right to maintain their proportional ownership in the company when new shares are issued. This means that if the company decides to issue additional shares, existing shareholders have the opportunity to purchase these shares before they are offered to external investors. Preemptive rights help protect existing shareholders from dilution of their ownership stake.

c. Liquidation Rights: In the event of the company's liquidation or winding-up, shareholders have the right to a portion of the company's assets. After satisfying the claims of creditors and other obligations, any remaining assets are distributed to shareholders according to their ownership percentage. Liquidation rights provide shareholders with a safeguard to recover their investment if the company ceases its operations.

5.2 Voting Rights:

a. Electing Directors: Shareholders have the right to vote to elect members of the board of directors. Directors are responsible for overseeing the company's management and making key decisions on behalf of shareholders. By participating in director elections, shareholders have a say in the composition of the board and can influence the company's strategic direction.

b.   Approving Major Decisions: Shareholders have the right to vote on significant matters that can impact the company's operations and structure. These may include approving mergers, acquisitions, major investments, amendments to the company's bylaws, or changes to the capital structure. By exercising their voting rights, shareholders can voice their opinions and influence important corporate decisions.

5.3 Information Rights:

a.   Financial Reporting: Shareholders have the right to receive accurate and timely financial information about the company. Companies are required to provide regular financial reports, including annual reports, quarterly statements, and audited financial statements. These reports provide shareholders with insights into the company's financial performance, its assets and liabilities, revenue and expenses, and other relevant financial data.

b.   Shareholder Meetings: Shareholders have the right to attend general meetings of the company, such as annual general meetings (AGMs) or extraordinary general meetings (EGMs). These meetings serve as a platform for shareholders to engage with the company's management, ask questions, and express their views on various matters, including the company's performance, strategy, and governance.

c.   Proxy Voting: Shareholders can appoint proxies to vote on their behalf in shareholder meetings. This allows shareholders who are unable to attend the meeting in person to still exercise their voting rights. Proxies are authorized individuals or entities who vote according to the instructions given by the shareholder. Proxy voting enables shareholders to participate in decision-making even if they cannot be physically present at the meeting.

It is important to note that shareholder rights may be subject to legal and regulatory requirements, as well as the company's bylaws and shareholder agreements. Shareholders should familiarize themselves with their rights and responsibilities and actively participate in corporate governance processes to protect their interests and contribute to the effective management of the company.

6. Legal Frameworks and Mechanisms for Protecting Shareholder Rights
    Various legal frameworks and mechanisms are in place to protect shareholder rights and ensure their fair treatment. These frameworks may differ across jurisdictions, but they generally aim to provide a level playing field for shareholders and promote transparency, accountability, and shareholder participation. Here are some key legal frameworks and mechanisms for protecting shareholder rights:

6.1 Company Laws and Corporate Governance Codes: Company laws establish the legal framework for corporations and outline the rights and responsibilities of shareholders. They provide rules for the formation, governance, and operation of companies. Corporate governance codes, on the other hand, provide guidelines and best practices for corporate governance, including the protection of shareholder rights. These laws and codes often address issues such as shareholder voting, disclosure requirements, board composition, and shareholder remedies.

6.2 Shareholder Voting Rights and Procedures: Laws and regulations typically grant shareholders the right to vote on important matters, such as the election of directors, mergers and acquisitions, and changes to the company's bylaws. These voting rights are essential for shareholder participation and influence. Mechanisms for protecting voting rights include requiring advance notice of meetings, ensuring transparency in the voting process, and allowing shareholders to appoint proxies to vote on their behalf.

6.3 Disclosure and Transparency Requirements: Shareholders have the right to access relevant and timely information about the company's operations, financial performance, and governance practices. Laws and regulations require companies to disclose financial statements, annual reports, and other material information to shareholders. These requirements ensure transparency and enable shareholders to make informed decisions and exercise their rights effectively.

6.4 Minority Shareholder Protections: Legal frameworks often provide specific protections for minority shareholders who may be at a disadvantage compared to controlling shareholders. These protections may include provisions against shareholder oppression, squeeze-outs, and discriminatory treatment. Minority shareholders may have rights to dissent, seek remedies for unfair practices, or challenge transactions that are detrimental to their interests.

6.5 Derivative Actions and Class Action Lawsuits: Shareholders may have the right to bring derivative actions or participate in class action lawsuits to protect their interests. These legal mechanisms allow shareholders to seek remedies on behalf of the company for actions that harm the company or its shareholders. Derivative actions involve shareholders suing on behalf of the company when the company's management fails to take appropriate action. Class action lawsuits enable shareholders to collectively seek redress for common grievances.

6.6 Shareholder Activism: Shareholder activism is a mechanism through which shareholders actively engage with companies to drive positive change.

Shareholders may use various strategies, such as engaging in dialogue with management, proposing shareholder resolutions, or nominating directors to the board. Laws and regulations may protect and facilitate shareholder activism, ensuring shareholders can exercise their rights to voice concerns and advocate for improvements in corporate practices.

6.7 Regulatory Oversight and Enforcement: Regulatory authorities, such as securities commissions or stock exchanges, play a vital role in overseeing corporate activities and enforcing compliance with shareholder rights protections. They may establish reporting requirements, investigate potential violations, and take enforcement actions against companies that fail to uphold shareholder rights or engage in unfair practices.

6.8 Independent Directors and Board Oversight: The presence of independent directors on the board can contribute to the protection of shareholder rights. Independent directors are expected to act in the best interests of the company and its shareholders as a whole, ensuring proper governance and oversight. They provide checks and balances, mitigate conflicts of interest, and help safeguard shareholder interests.

6.9 Shareholder Education and Engagement: Educating shareholders about their rights and providing avenues for engagement can empower shareholders to protect their interests. Companies may hold investor education programs, provide informative materials, and establish shareholder communication channels to foster dialogue and enhance shareholder participation.

6.10 Shareholder Agreements and Voting Trusts: Shareholders may enter into agreements that govern their relationships, protect their rights, and outline mechanisms for dispute resolution. Shareholder agreements can reinforce and enhance shareholder protections beyond what is mandated by law. Additionally, voting trusts allow shareholders to consolidate their voting power and collectively exercise their rights to influence corporate decisions.

It is important for shareholders to familiarize themselves with the legal frameworks and mechanisms available in their jurisdiction to protect their rights effectively. Shareholders should exercise their rights responsibly, stay informed about developments within the company, and seek legal advice if they believe their rights have been violated or compromised.

7. Shareholder Lawsuits and Class Actions

Shareholder lawsuits and class actions are legal mechanisms that allow shareholders to seek remedies for perceived violations of their rights or harm caused by a company's actions or omissions. These legal actions can be an important tool for shareholders to hold companies and their management accountable. Here's an overview of shareholder lawsuits and class actions:

7.1 Shareholder Lawsuits: Shareholder lawsuits, also known as shareholder litigation or derivative actions, are legal actions initiated by individual shareholders on behalf of the company against directors, officers, or other parties alleged to have harmed the company. These lawsuits typically arise when management fails to take action to address alleged misconduct or when they breach their fiduciary duties to the company and its shareholders. Shareholder lawsuits seek to recover damages or obtain equitable relief for the company.

Key aspects of shareholder lawsuits include:
• Standing: Shareholders generally need to demonstrate that they have standing to bring a lawsuit on behalf of the company. This often requires showing that they owned shares at the time of the alleged wrongdoing and that they have made a demand on the company's board of directors to take action or that such demand would be futile.
• Fiduciary Duty Claims: Shareholder lawsuits often involve claims that directors or officers breached their fiduciary duties, such as the duty of loyalty or the duty of care, by engaging in self-dealing, mismanagement, fraud, or other wrongful acts.
• Damage Recovery: Shareholder lawsuits may seek monetary damages to compensate the company for losses caused by the alleged wrongdoing. In some cases, they may also seek injunctive relief, such as court orders to halt certain actions or force specific actions.
• Settlements: Shareholder lawsuits often result in settlements, where the parties reach an agreement to resolve the claims without a court ruling. Settlements may involve monetary compensation, changes to corporate governance practices, or other remedies deemed appropriate.
• Court Approval: In many jurisdictions, shareholder lawsuits and settlements require court approval to ensure fairness and protect the interests of shareholders.

7.2 Class Actions: Class actions are lawsuits brought on behalf of a group or class of shareholders who have suffered similar harm. In class actions, one or more shareholders act as representatives for the class, consolidating their claims into a single lawsuit. Class actions can be particularly effective when numerous shareholders have relatively small individual claims that would be impractical to pursue individually.

Key aspects of class actions include:
• Certification: Courts typically need to certify a class action, ensuring that the claims and issues are sufficiently similar and that the representative

plaintiff adequately represents the class members.

• Notice and Opt-Out: Class members are usually provided with notice of the lawsuit and have the option to opt-out, meaning they choose not to be part of the class action and pursue their claims individually.

• Settlements and Judgments: If a class action is successful, a settlement or judgment may result in compensation for the class members. The distribution of funds among class members is usually determined by the court, taking into account individual losses or other relevant factors.

• Legal Fees: In class actions, attorneys often work on a contingency fee basis, meaning they only receive compensation if the lawsuit is successful or a settlement is reached. Legal fees are typically subject to court approval to ensure they are reasonable and proportionate.

Shareholder lawsuits and class actions can provide shareholders with a means to seek redress and protect their interests when they believe their rights have been violated. However, it is important to note that these legal actions can be complex, time-consuming, and costly. Shareholders should consult with legal professionals experienced in shareholder litigation to evaluate the merits of their case and understand the potential risks and benefits of pursuing legal action.

8. Importance of Shareholder Engagement
8.1 Enhancing Corporate Governance
• Active shareholder engagement promotes better corporate governance practices.
• Engaged shareholders can contribute to board diversity, responsible executive compensation, and effective risk management.
8.2 Encouraging Sustainable Business Practices
• Shareholders can use their influence to encourage companies to adopt environmentally and socially responsible practices.
• Shareholder resolutions and engagement can drive positive change on issues such as climate change, human rights, and diversity.
8.3 Protecting Shareholder Value
• Shareholder engagement helps protect shareholder value by holding management accountable and preventing self-serving actions.
• Active shareholders can raise concerns, propose improvements, and help safeguard the long-term interests of the company and its shareholders.

9. Summary
Shareholders play a crucial role as vital stakeholders in a company, holding ownership rights that give them a vested interest in its success. By investing their capital and becoming shareholders, individuals and entities become part-owners of the company and gain the right to participate in its decision-making processes. Recognizing and protecting shareholder rights is essential

for maintaining a fair and transparent corporate environment. Shareholder rights provide a framework for accountability and ensure that the interests of shareholders are aligned with the long-term goals and sustainability of the company.

Recognizing shareholder rights fosters transparency within the company. Shareholders have the right to access accurate and timely information about the company's financial performance, corporate governance practices, and strategic plans. This access to information allows shareholders to make informed decisions and evaluate the company's performance. Transparency enables shareholders to hold management accountable and contributes to the overall integrity and trustworthiness of the company. When shareholders are well-informed, they can actively engage in discussions, ask relevant questions, and provide valuable insights to shape the company's direction.

Moreover, protecting shareholder rights promotes accountability within the company. Shareholders have the right to vote on critical matters, such as the election of directors and major business decisions. This voting power ensures that shareholders have a voice in key corporate decisions and can influence the governance and strategic direction of the company. By actively participating in voting processes, shareholders can hold management accountable for their actions and decisions. This accountability helps prevent self-interested behavior, encourages responsible decision-making, and safeguards the long-term interests of the company and its shareholders.

Engaged shareholders are essential contributors to the overall success of a company. Their active participation in corporate affairs brings diverse perspectives, expertise, and knowledge to the table. Engaged shareholders often engage in constructive dialogue with management, provide feedback, and offer suggestions for improvement. Their involvement can enhance corporate governance practices, promote ethical behavior, and drive sustainable practices. By exercising their rights and responsibilities, engaged shareholders contribute to building stronger, more resilient companies that create value for shareholders and stakeholders alike.

Thus, shareholders hold ownership rights and responsibilities that make them vital stakeholders in a company. Recognizing and protecting shareholder rights ensures transparency, accountability, and sustainable corporate practices. Engaged shareholders actively participate in decision-making processes, contribute to the company's success, and play a pivotal role in shaping its governance and strategic direction. By providing a platform for transparency, accountability, and active engagement, shareholder rights contribute to the overall integrity and long-term sustainability of the company.

References

1.   Aguilera, R. V., Desender, K. A., Bednar, M. K., & Lee, J. H. (2015). Connecting the dots: Bringing external corporate governance into the

corporate governance puzzle. Academy of Management Annals, 9(1), 483-573.

2.   Allen, F., & Gale, D. (2000). Corporate governance and competition. NBER working paper, No. 7627.

3.   Becht, M., Bolton, P., & Röell, A. (2011). Why bank governance is different. Oxford Review of Economic Policy, 27(3), 437-463.

4.   Black, B. S., & Carvalho, A. G. (2018). The diverse objectives of sovereign wealth funds: A legal perspective. The Journal of Economic Perspectives, 32(3), 175-198.

5.   Coffee Jr, J. C. (2001). The rise of dispersed ownership: The role of law in the separation of ownership and control. Yale Law Journal, 111(1), 1-82.

6.   Coffee Jr, J. C. (2012). Corporate governance and social responsibility in a comparative perspective. Columbia Law Review, 112(6), 1535-1624.

7.   Davis, G. F., & Thompson, T. (1994). A social movement perspective on corporate control. Administrative Science Quarterly, 39(1), 141-173.

8.   Fama, E. F., & Jensen, M. C. (1983). Separation of ownership and control. Journal of Law and Economics, 26(2), 301-325.

9.   Gilson, R. J., & Gordon, J. N. (2003). Controlling shareholders and corporate governance: Complicating the comparative taxonomy. Journal of Comparative Economics, 31(4), 725-746.

10. Hansmann, H., & Kraakman, R. (2001). The end of history for corporate law. Georgetown Law Journal, 89, 439-468.

11. Hermalin, B. E., & Weisbach, M. S. (2011). Information disclosure and corporate governance. Journal of Finance, 66(2), 195-224.

12. Hillman, A. J., & Dalziel, T. (2003). Boards of directors and firm performance: Integrating agency and resource dependence perspectives. Academy of Management Review, 28(3), 383-396.

13. Jensen, M. C., & Meckling, W. H. (1976). Theory of the firm: Managerial behavior, agency costs and ownership structure. Journal of Financial Economics, 3(4), 305-360.

14. La Porta, R., Lopez-de-Silanes, F., Shleifer, A., & Vishny, R. W. (1997). Legal determinants of external finance. Journal of Finance, 52(3), 1131-1150.

15. Lipton, M., & Lorsch, J. W. (1992). A modest proposal for improved corporate governance. Business Lawyer, 48(1), 59-77.

16. Macey, J. R. (2008). Corporate governance: Promises kept, promises broken. Princeton University Press.

17. Mallin, C. A. (2016). Corporate governance. Oxford University Press.

18. Monks, R. A., & Minow, N. (2011). Corporate governance. John

Wiley & Sons.

19. Pistor, K. (2013). Comparative corporate governance: Legal perspectives. Columbia Law Review, 113(4), 889-934.

20. Roe, M. J. (2003). Political determinants of corporate governance: Political context, corporate impact. Oxford Review of Economic Policy, 19(2), 211-227.

21. Shleifer, A., & Vishny, R. W. (1997). A survey of corporate governance. Journal of Finance, 52(2), 737-783.

22. Stout, L. A. (2012). The shareholder value myth: How putting shareholders first harms investors, corporations, and the public. Berrett-Koehler Publishers.

23. Sundaramurthy, C., & Lewis, M. W. (2003). Control and collaboration: Paradoxes of governance. Academy of Management Review, 28(3), 397-415.

24. Tricker, R. I. (2015). Corporate governance: Principles, policies, and practices. Oxford University Press.

25. Yermack, D. (2017). Corporate governance and blockchains. Review of Finance, 21(1), 7-31.

CHAPTER 5
DISCLOSURE AND TRANSPARENCY IN CORPORATE GOVERNANCE
Dr. Navdeep Kaur[5]

Chapter Abstract

In today's dynamic business environment, corporate governance plays a crucial role in ensuring the accountability, integrity, and sustainability of organizations. Transparency and disclosure are key principles that underpin effective corporate governance, providing stakeholders with the information they need to make informed decisions. This chapter explores the importance of disclosure and transparency in corporate governance, the benefits they offer, and the practices that promote them.

1. Defining Disclosure and Transparency

1.1 Understanding Disclosure: Disclosure refers to the process of providing accurate, relevant, and timely information about a company's financial, operational, and governance activities to its stakeholders. It enables stakeholders to assess a company's performance, risk profile, and decision-making processes.

1.2 Understanding Transparency: Transparency refers to the openness, clarity, and accessibility of information. Transparent corporate governance ensures that relevant information is available to stakeholders, promoting accountability, trust, and ethical behavior.

2. The Importance of Disclosure and Transparency in Corporate Governance

---

[5] Associate Professor, School of Management Studies, CT University, Ludhiana

Disclosure and transparency are of utmost importance in corporate governance for several reasons:

2.1 Building Trust and Confidence: Disclosure and transparency help build trust among stakeholders, including shareholders, investors, employees, customers, and the public. When companies provide clear and reliable information about their activities, performance, and decision-making processes, stakeholders gain confidence in the organization's operations and governance practices. This trust is essential for attracting investment, retaining talented employees, and maintaining a positive reputation.

2.2 Informed Decision-making: Transparent disclosure allows stakeholders to make informed decisions. Investors rely on accurate and comprehensive information to assess the financial health, performance, and risks associated with an organization. Employees can evaluate the stability and sustainability of their jobs. Customers can assess the quality and safety of products or services. Transparent disclosure empowers stakeholders to make well-informed choices based on reliable data, reducing uncertainties and minimizing potential risks.

2.3 Mitigating Agency Problems: Agency problems arise when the interests of managers and shareholders diverge. Transparent disclosure helps align these interests by reducing information asymmetry between management and shareholders. When shareholders have access to relevant and timely information, they can monitor management's actions, evaluate performance, and hold executives accountable. This oversight helps mitigate agency problems, reducing the likelihood of self-serving behavior and enhancing the organization's governance effectiveness.

2.4 Regulatory Compliance: Disclosure and transparency play a crucial role in meeting legal and regulatory requirements. Governments and regulatory bodies enforce specific disclosure obligations to protect investors, ensure fair competition, and maintain market integrity. By adhering to these requirements and providing accurate information, organizations demonstrate their commitment to ethical practices, avoid legal repercussions, and foster a compliant corporate culture.

2.5 Stakeholder Engagement: Transparent disclosure facilitates effective communication and engagement with stakeholders. By sharing information on corporate strategy, performance, and governance practices, companies foster a sense of inclusiveness and openness. This engagement allows stakeholders to provide feedback, voice concerns, and contribute to the decision-making process. The dialogue between companies and stakeholders builds stronger relationships, enhances trust, and promotes the alignment of interests.

2.6 Risk Management: Transparent disclosure of risks and risk management practices is essential for effective risk management. By disclosing material risks, organizations provide stakeholders with a clear understanding of the potential challenges they face. This information enables stakeholders to assess risk appetite, evaluate risk mitigation strategies, and make informed decisions regarding their involvement with the organization. Transparent risk disclosure fosters a proactive approach to risk management and enhances the organization's resilience in the face of uncertainties.

2.7 Long-term Sustainability: Disclosure and transparency contribute to the long-term sustainability of organizations. By providing stakeholders with information on environmental, social, and governance (ESG) factors, companies demonstrate their commitment to responsible and sustainable practices. Stakeholders increasingly consider ESG performance when making investment decisions, purchasing products, or choosing to work with or for a company. Transparent disclosure of ESG metrics allows organizations to attract socially conscious investors, maintain positive relationships with customers and employees, and build a resilient and future-proof business model.

In conclusion, disclosure and transparency are vital components of effective corporate governance. They foster trust, enable informed decision-making, mitigate agency problems, ensure regulatory compliance, engage stakeholders, enhance risk management, and promote long-term sustainability. Organizations that prioritize and embrace transparency and disclosure practices create a solid foundation for ethical conduct, accountability, and stakeholder value creation.

3. Financial Reporting and Disclosures

Financial reporting and disclosures are essential aspects of disclosure and transparency in corporate governance. Companies are required to provide accurate and reliable financial statements, including balance sheets, income statements, cash flow statements, and accompanying notes. These financial reports provide stakeholders with insights into the organization's financial performance, position, and cash flows.

To ensure transparency, companies must adhere to recognized accounting standards, such as Generally Accepted Accounting Principles (GAAP) or International Financial Reporting Standards (IFRS). Adhering to these standards promotes consistency, comparability, and reliability in financial reporting across different organizations and jurisdictions.

In addition to the financial statements, companies should disclose relevant information in the footnotes or management discussion and analysis (MD&A) section of their reports. This includes details about accounting policies, significant judgments and estimates, related-party transactions, contingencies, and other relevant information that could impact stakeholders' understanding of the financial statements.

4. Auditing and Assurance and Disclosures

Auditing and assurance play a crucial role in ensuring the accuracy and reliability of financial reporting. Independent external auditors examine the company's financial statements and assess whether they present a true and fair view of the organization's financial position and performance.

Through the audit process, auditors evaluate the internal controls, test the completeness and accuracy of financial information, and express an opinion on the fairness of the financial statements. This independent verification enhances stakeholders' confidence in the reliability of the disclosed information.

Transparent corporate governance involves selecting competent and independent auditors, maintaining open communication with auditors, and addressing any identified deficiencies or weaknesses in internal controls or financial reporting processes. Regular audits provide assurance to stakeholders that the company's financial information is accurate and trustworthy.

5. Role of Information Technology

Information technology (IT) plays a significant role in facilitating disclosure and transparency in corporate governance. IT systems enable companies to collect, process, store, and disseminate information efficiently and effectively.

Robust IT infrastructure supports the timely and accurate preparation of financial reports, ensuring data integrity and minimizing the risk of errors or manipulation. Companies can implement enterprise resource planning (ERP) systems, financial management software, and reporting tools to streamline financial processes and generate reliable and consistent information.

Furthermore, technology enables organizations to enhance transparency by providing stakeholders with access to information through digital platforms. Investor portals, corporate websites, and online reporting tools can be utilized to share financial statements, annual reports, governance policies, and other relevant disclosures in an accessible and user-friendly manner.

6. Corporate Social Responsibility (CSR) Reporting

Corporate social responsibility (CSR) reporting focuses on the disclosure of a company's environmental, social, and governance (ESG) practices and performance. It goes beyond financial reporting to provide stakeholders with information on the company's impact on society, the environment, and its commitment to ethical practices.

CSR reporting involves disclosing information related to environmental stewardship, social initiatives, employee well-being, supply chain management, diversity and inclusion, community engagement, and other sustainability-related activities. This information allows stakeholders to evaluate the company's commitment to responsible business practices and its contribution to sustainable development.

Transparent CSR reporting provides stakeholders with insights into the company's values, priorities, and long-term sustainability strategy. It helps investors make socially responsible investment decisions, customers make ethical purchasing choices, and employees align themselves with organizations that share their values.

Thus, expanding on disclosure and transparency in corporate governance includes focusing on financial reporting and disclosures, auditing and assurance, the role of information technology, and corporate social responsibility reporting. These elements enhance the reliability of financial information, provide independent verification, utilize technology for efficient information dissemination, and promote responsible and sustainable practices. By embracing these aspects, companies can create a transparent and accountable governance framework that instills trust, fosters stakeholder engagement, and contributes to long-term value creation.

7. Summary

Disclosure and transparency serve as the bedrock of effective corporate governance by fostering stakeholder confidence. When companies are transparent in their operations and disclose relevant information, stakeholders, including investors, employees, and customers, gain a sense of trust and assurance. Transparent disclosure allows investors to make informed investment decisions based on accurate and reliable information about the company's financial health and performance. Employees feel secure when they have access to transparent information about the organization's strategies, goals, and policies, enabling them to align their aspirations and commitments. Similarly, customers value transparency as it helps them evaluate the quality, safety, and ethical standards of products or services. By prioritizing disclosure and transparency, organizations can cultivate stakeholder confidence, leading to stronger relationships, increased loyalty, and enhanced reputation.

Moreover, disclosure and transparency play a crucial role in enabling informed decision-making. By providing stakeholders with comprehensive and timely information, organizations empower them to make well-informed choices. Investors can assess the risks and potential returns associated with their investment decisions, leading to more efficient capital allocation. Employees can evaluate the stability and sustainability of their jobs, enabling them to make career decisions based on reliable information. Customers can assess the value proposition and ethical standards of companies, allowing them to make purchasing decisions aligned with their preferences and values. Informed decision-making across stakeholders promotes better outcomes, reduces uncertainties, and minimizes risks. By embracing disclosure and transparency, organizations facilitate the flow of relevant information, enabling stakeholders to make decisions with confidence and contributing to overall market efficiency and effectiveness.

References

1. Adams, R., & Mehran, H. (2012). Corporate performance, governance, and shareholder activism. Journal of Corporate Finance, 18(1), 177-195.

2. Aggarwal, R., Erel, I., Ferreira, M. A., & Matos, P. (2011). Does governance travel around the world? Evidence from institutional investors. Journal of Financial Economics, 100(1), 154-181.

3. Bebchuk, L. A., Cohen, A., & Ferrell, A. (2009). What matters in corporate governance? The Review of Financial Studies, 22(2), 783-827.

4. Becht, M., Bolton, P., & Roell, A. (2005). Corporate governance and control. Handbook of Corporate Finance: Empirical Corporate Finance, 1, 1-109.

5. Coffee Jr, J. C. (2006). The future as history: The prospects for global convergence in corporate governance and its implications. Northwestern University Law Review, 100, 607-669.

6. Daily, C. M., Dalton, D. R., & Cannella Jr, A. A. (2003). Corporate governance: Decades of dialogue and data. Academy of Management Review, 28(3), 371-382.

7. Fama, E. F., & Jensen, M. C. (1983). Separation of ownership and control. The Journal of Law and Economics, 26(2), 301-325.

8. Gillan, S. L., & Starks, L. T. (2003). Corporate governance, corporate ownership, and the role of institutional investors: A global perspective. Journal of Applied Finance, 13(2), 4-22.

9. Hermalin, B. E., & Weisbach, M. S. (2003). Boards of directors as an endogenously determined institution: A survey of the economic literature. Economic Policy Review, 9(1), 7-26.

10. Jensen, M. C., & Meckling, W. H. (1976). Theory of the firm: Managerial behavior, agency costs and ownership structure. Journal of Financial Economics, 3(4), 305-360.

11. La Porta, R., Lopez-de-Silanes, F., & Shleifer, A. (2006). What works in securities laws? The Journal of Finance, 61(1), 1-32.

12. La Porta, R., Lopez-de-Silanes, F., Shleifer, A., & Vishny, R. (2000). Investor protection and corporate governance. The Journal of Financial Economics, 58(1-2), 3-27.

13. Mallin, C. A. (2017). Corporate governance. Oxford University Press.

14. Monks, R. A., & Minow, N. (2011). Corporate governance. John

Wiley & Sons.

15. OECD. (2015). G20/OECD Principles of Corporate Governance. Paris: OECD Publishing.

16. Shleifer, A., & Vishny, R. W. (1997). A survey of corporate governance. The Journal of Finance, 52(2), 737-783.

17. Tirole, J. (2001). Corporate governance. Econometrica, 69(1), 1-35.

18. Tricker, R. I. (2015). Corporate governance: Principles, policies, and practices. Oxford University Press.

19. Williamson, O. E. (1985). The economic institutions of capitalism: Firms, markets, relational contracting. New York: The Free Press.

20. Yermack, D. (2017). Corporate governance and blockchains. Review of Finance, 21(1), 7-31.

CHAPTER 6
RISK MANAGEMENT AND INTERNAL CONTROLS
Dr. Kangan Sayal[6]

Chapter Abstract

In today's complex and rapidly changing business environment, organizations face a multitude of risks that can impact their operations, financial stability, and reputation. Risk management and internal controls play a vital role in helping organizations identify, assess, and mitigate these risks. This chapter explores the concepts of risk management and internal controls, their importance in business operations, and how they work together to safeguard organizational assets and achieve strategic objectives.

1. Understanding Risk Management

Risk management is the process of identifying, analyzing, and responding to risks to minimize their potential impact on an organization. It involves a systematic approach to assess both internal and external risks, evaluate their likelihood and potential consequences, and develop strategies to manage and mitigate them. Effective risk management helps organizations make informed decisions, allocate resources efficiently, and protect their interests.

1.1 Types of Risks

Risks can be classified into various types based on their nature, origin, or impact on an organization. Understanding these different types of risks helps organizations identify and address potential threats effectively. Here are some common types of risks:

1.1.1 Strategic Risks: Strategic risks relate to uncertainties in achieving an organization's strategic objectives. They arise from external factors such as

---

[6] Assistant Professor, School of Management Studies, CT University, Ludhiana

changes in market dynamics, competitive landscape, technological advancements, or shifts in customer preferences. Strategic risks can also stem from internal factors such as ineffective strategic planning, poor decision-making, or inadequate resource allocation.

Examples: Entry of a new competitor, changes in government regulations, disruptive technologies, shifts in consumer behavior, economic downturns.

1.1.2 Operational Risks: Operational risks arise from day-to-day business operations and processes. They are associated with failures or inefficiencies in operational procedures, systems, or people. Operational risks can lead to disruptions in business activities, financial losses, reputational damage, or non-compliance with regulations.

Examples: Equipment breakdown, supply chain disruptions, human errors, process inefficiencies, cybersecurity breaches, product defects, fraud.

1.1.3 Financial Risks: Financial risks pertain to potential losses resulting from financial transactions or investments. These risks can impact an organization's financial stability, profitability, and cash flow. Financial risks include market risks, credit risks, liquidity risks, and currency risks.

Examples: Fluctuations in exchange rates, interest rate changes, credit defaults, market volatility, inadequate cash flow, financial fraud.

1.1.4 Compliance Risks: Compliance risks involve the failure to adhere to laws, regulations, industry standards, or internal policies and procedures. Non-compliance can result in legal penalties, reputational damage, loss of licenses or certifications, and operational disruptions.

Examples: Regulatory violations, non-compliance with data privacy laws, failure to meet industry standards, non-adherence to internal control procedures, breaches of codes of conduct.

1.1.5 Reputational Risks: Reputational risks relate to the potential damage to an organization's reputation, brand image, or public perception. These risks can arise from negative publicity, customer complaints, product recalls, ethical misconduct, or social media backlash.

Examples: Product recalls, public scandals, data breaches, negative customer reviews, environmental controversies, executive misconduct.

1.1.6 Environmental and Sustainability Risks: Environmental and sustainability risks arise from the impact of an organization's activities on the environment and society. These risks include ecological damage, climate change, resource scarcity, and non-compliance with environmental regulations.

Examples: Pollution incidents, carbon emissions, natural disasters, resource depletion, regulatory changes related to sustainability.

2. Risk Identification and Assessment

Risk identification and assessment are crucial components of the risk management process. They involve systematically identifying potential risks, analyzing their characteristics, and evaluating their potential impact on the organization. This detailed analysis helps organizations prioritize and develop strategies to effectively manage and mitigate risks. Let's delve into the process of risk identification and assessment in more detail:

2.1 Risk Identification: Risk identification is the process of systematically identifying and documenting potential risks that could impact the achievement of organizational objectives. This process involves engaging stakeholders, conducting thorough analyses, and utilizing various techniques to ensure a comprehensive identification of risks. Here are some key steps in the risk identification process:

a) Engage Stakeholders: Involve relevant stakeholders from different levels and departments of the organization to gather diverse perspectives and insights. This can include executives, managers, employees, customers, suppliers, and industry experts.

b) Review Organizational Documentation: Examine existing organizational documentation such as policies, procedures, financial statements, incident reports, and performance data. These documents can provide valuable information about past and potential risks.

c) Brainstorming and Workshops: Conduct brainstorming sessions or workshops with stakeholders to encourage open discussions and generate a wide range of potential risks. This can be done using techniques like mind mapping, SWOT analysis (Strengths, Weaknesses, Opportunities, and Threats), or scenario analysis.

d) Analyze Industry and External Factors: Evaluate industry trends, market conditions, regulatory changes, technological advancements, and other external factors that can impact the organization. This analysis helps identify risks associated with the external environment.

e) Internal Process Analysis: Examine each department's processes, activities, and systems to identify potential risks. This can include process flowcharts, control assessments, and review of historical incidents or near misses.

f) Risk Registers and Checklists: Utilize risk registers and checklists to ensure a systematic and comprehensive approach to risk identification. These tools can provide a structured framework for capturing and categorizing potential risks.

2.2 Risk Assessment: Risk assessment involves analyzing and evaluating identified risks to understand their characteristics, potential impact, and likelihood of occurrence. This assessment helps prioritize risks based on their significance, allowing organizations to allocate resources effectively. Here are key steps in the risk assessment process:

a) Risk Categorization: Group identified risks into categories based on their nature, such as strategic, operational, financial, compliance, or reputational risks. This categorization facilitates a better understanding and analysis of risks.

b) Risk Impact Analysis: Assess the potential impact of each risk on the organization's objectives, operations, financial stability, and reputation. Consider both quantitative and qualitative factors, such as financial loss, customer dissatisfaction, legal implications, or disruption of business operations.

c) Likelihood Assessment: Evaluate the likelihood or probability of each identified risk occurring. This assessment can be based on historical data, expert judgment, statistical analysis, or industry benchmarks. The likelihood assessment helps gauge the frequency or chance of a risk event occurring.

d) Risk Severity and Prioritization: Combine the impact and likelihood assessments to determine the overall severity or significance of each risk. Prioritize risks based on their severity to focus resources on the most critical risks that require immediate attention.

e) Risk Mitigation Strategies: Identify and develop strategies to manage and mitigate the prioritized risks. These strategies can include risk avoidance, risk reduction through controls or process changes, risk transfer through insurance or outsourcing, or risk acceptance if the cost of mitigation outweighs the potential impact.

f) Risk Register and Documentation: Maintain a risk register that documents the identified risks, their assessments, and the corresponding risk mitigation strategies. This register serves as a reference for ongoing risk management and helps track the effectiveness of risk mitigation efforts.

By systematically identifying and assessing risks, organizations gain a comprehensive understanding of the potential threats they face. This enables them to make informed decisions, allocate resources effectively, and implement appropriate risk mitigation measures. Regular reviews and updates of the risk identification and assessment process ensure that new risks are identified and managed, contributing to effective risk management practices within the organization.

3. Internal Controls and Compliance

Internal controls and compliance are closely intertwined concepts that help organizations ensure adherence to laws, regulations, and internal policies. Internal controls provide a framework for managing and mitigating risks, while compliance ensures that the organization operates within legal and ethical boundaries. Let's discuss internal controls and compliance in detail:

3.1 Internal Controls: Internal controls refer to the policies, procedures, and practices established by an organization to provide reasonable assurance regarding the achievement of objectives, effectiveness and efficiency of operations, reliability of financial reporting, and compliance with laws and regulations. Here are some key aspects of internal controls:

a) Control Environment: The control environment sets the tone at the top of the organization. It includes the organization's ethical values, management's commitment to integrity, and the overall culture of control consciousness.

b) Risk Assessment: Internal controls are designed to address identified risks. Risk assessment involves identifying and evaluating risks to determine their potential impact on achieving objectives. This assessment helps organizations prioritize and allocate resources effectively.

c) Control Activities: Control activities are policies and procedures implemented to mitigate identified risks. These activities can be preventive, detective, or corrective in nature. Examples include segregation of duties, authorization and approval processes, physical safeguards, and information technology controls.

d) Information and Communication: Internal controls ensure the accuracy, reliability, and timely communication of information. Reliable information is crucial for decision-making and monitoring organizational performance. Effective communication ensures that relevant information reaches the appropriate stakeholders.

e) Monitoring: Continuous monitoring ensures that internal controls are functioning effectively. It involves ongoing reviews, assessments, and audits to identify control deficiencies, assess the reliability of financial reporting, and take corrective actions as needed.

3.2 Compliance: Compliance refers to an organization's adherence to laws, regulations, industry standards, and internal policies. Compliance ensures that the organization operates ethically, avoids legal penalties, protects its reputation, and fosters trust among stakeholders. Here are some key aspects of compliance:

a) Regulatory Compliance: Organizations must comply with laws and regulations relevant to their industry and operations. These can include labor laws, environmental regulations, data privacy laws, financial reporting standards, and consumer protection laws. Compliance often involves understanding and interpreting complex regulations, implementing controls to meet requirements, and maintaining documentation.

b) Internal Policy Compliance: Organizations establish internal policies and procedures to guide employees' behavior and ensure consistency in operations. These policies cover areas such as code of conduct, financial controls, procurement, information security, and human resources. Compliance with internal policies helps maintain consistency, transparency, and accountability within the organization.

c) Compliance Monitoring and Reporting: Organizations need to monitor compliance with laws, regulations, and internal policies regularly. This involves conducting internal audits, reviews, and assessments to identify areas of non-compliance, control deficiencies, or potential risks. Compliance reporting ensures that relevant stakeholders, including management, board of directors, and regulatory bodies, are informed about the organization's compliance status.

d) Compliance Training and Awareness: Organizations must provide training and awareness programs to educate employees about applicable laws, regulations, and internal policies. This helps employees understand their responsibilities, the consequences of non-compliance, and promotes a culture of compliance throughout the organization.

e) Regulatory Reporting and Disclosure: Compliance often involves reporting obligations to regulatory bodies, such as financial statements, tax filings, environmental reports, and disclosures of material events. Organizations need to ensure accurate and timely reporting to maintain compliance with regulatory requirements.

The integration of internal controls and compliance ensures that risks are identified and managed effectively, and the organization operates within legal and ethical boundaries. It helps protect the organization's assets, ensures reliable financial reporting, and fosters trust among stakeholders. Regular monitoring and assessments of internal controls and compliance activities are essential to identify areas of improvement, address control deficiencies, and adapt to changing regulatory environments.

4. Fraud prevention and Whistleblower Mechanisms

Fraud prevention and whistleblower mechanisms are crucial components of an organization's efforts to detect and prevent fraudulent activities. Fraud can cause significant financial losses, damage to reputation, and legal implications for organizations. Implementing effective fraud prevention measures and establishing a robust whistleblower mechanism can help organizations detect and address fraud in a timely manner. Let's discuss fraud prevention and whistleblower mechanisms in more detail:

4.1 Fraud Prevention: Fraud prevention involves implementing proactive measures to reduce the risk of fraudulent activities occurring within an organization. Here are key elements of a comprehensive fraud prevention program:

a) Fraud Risk Assessment: Conduct a thorough assessment of the organization's vulnerabilities to fraud. Identify potential fraud risks based on the organization's industry, operations, processes, and external factors. This assessment helps prioritize areas that require enhanced controls and monitoring.

b) Strong Internal Controls: Establish and enforce internal controls to mitigate fraud risks. Internal controls can include segregation of duties, authorization and approval processes, regular reconciliations, physical safeguards, access controls, and IT security measures. These controls help prevent and detect fraudulent activities by providing checks and balances.

c) Ethical Culture and Tone at the Top: Promote an ethical culture within the organization, starting from the top leadership. Management should emphasize the importance of integrity, ethics, and compliance with laws and regulations. Clear communication of organizational values and ethical expectations sets the tone for employees to act ethically and report suspicious activities.

d) Fraud Awareness and Training: Provide training and awareness programs to employees about different types of fraud, red flags, and reporting mechanisms. Educate employees on their roles and responsibilities in preventing and detecting fraud. Training can include examples of fraudulent schemes, ethical decision-making, and the consequences of fraud.

e) Regular Monitoring and Auditing: Conduct regular monitoring and internal audits to detect anomalies, identify control weaknesses, and assess compliance with policies and procedures. Monitoring activities can include data analytics, transactional reviews, surprise audits, and proactive detection techniques. These activities help identify potential fraud indicators and enable prompt action.

f) Anti-Fraud Policies and Procedures: Develop and communicate anti-fraud policies and procedures that clearly outline expectations, reporting mechanisms, and disciplinary actions. Policies should address areas such as conflicts of interest, gifts and entertainment, vendor management, and expense reimbursements. Regularly review and update these policies to adapt to evolving fraud risks.

4.2 Whistleblower Mechanisms: Whistleblower mechanisms provide channels for employees and stakeholders to report suspected fraudulent activities or unethical behavior confidentially and without fear of retaliation. Here are key considerations for establishing effective whistleblower mechanisms:

a) Confidentiality and Anonymity: Ensure that whistleblowers can report concerns confidentially and, if desired, anonymously. Confidentiality protects the identity of the whistleblower and encourages reporting without fear of reprisal.

b) Multiple Reporting Channels: Establish multiple reporting channels to accommodate different preferences and comfort levels of whistleblowers. Channels can include dedicated hotlines, email, web-based reporting systems, and even physical drop boxes. Provide clear instructions on how to access and use these channels.

c) Non-Retaliation Policies: Implement robust non-retaliation policies that protect whistleblowers from any form of retaliation for reporting in good faith. Assure whistleblowers that their identities will be kept confidential and that appropriate action will be taken against retaliation.

d) Investigation and Follow-up: Establish a clear process for investigating reported concerns. Designate a responsible party or a specialized team to handle investigations objectively and promptly. Ensure that whistleblowers are provided with feedback on the progress and outcome of the investigations, while maintaining confidentiality.

e) Communication and Awareness: Promote awareness of the whistleblower mechanism within the organization through training programs, communication campaigns, and regular reminders. Employees should understand the importance of reporting and feel confident in the process.

f) Documentation and Reporting: Maintain detailed records of reported concerns, investigations, and outcomes. Track and analyze reported incidents to identify patterns, trends, and areas of improvement in fraud prevention efforts.

By implementing robust fraud prevention measures and establishing effective whistleblower mechanisms, organizations create a culture of transparency, integrity, and accountability. This enables early detection and timely response to fraudulent activities, ultimately reducing the financial and reputational impact on the organization.

5. Business Continuity Planning

Business continuity planning (BCP) is a proactive process that helps organizations prepare for and respond to potential disruptions, crises, or disasters. It involves developing strategies, procedures, and resources to ensure that critical business functions can continue or be rapidly restored in the event of an adverse event. Business continuity planning aims to minimize downtime, protect assets, and maintain essential operations to meet the needs of stakeholders. Let's discuss business continuity planning in more detail:

5.1 Risk Assessment: The first step in business continuity planning is conducting a comprehensive risk assessment. This involves identifying potential risks and assessing their potential impact on the organization. Risks can include natural disasters, technology failures, cybersecurity threats, pandemics, supply chain disruptions, or any event that could disrupt normal business operations. The risk assessment helps prioritize planning efforts and allocate resources effectively.

5.2 Business Impact Analysis (BIA): A business impact analysis is conducted to assess the potential financial, operational, and reputational impacts of disruptions on critical business functions. It involves identifying critical processes, dependencies, and recovery time objectives (RTOs) for each function. The BIA helps organizations understand the prioritization of recovery efforts and allocate resources accordingly.

5.3 Strategy Development: Based on the risk assessment and business impact analysis, organizations develop strategies and plans to ensure business continuity. These strategies typically include:

a) Emergency Response Plan: Establishing an emergency response plan outlines immediate actions to be taken in the event of an incident. It includes procedures for evacuations, medical emergencies, communications, and emergency contacts.

b) Crisis Management Plan: A crisis management plan outlines the organizational structure, roles, and responsibilities of key personnel during a crisis. It includes communication protocols, decision-making processes, and coordination mechanisms to effectively manage the crisis response.

c) Business Recovery Plan: This plan focuses on restoring critical business functions and operations. It includes procedures for relocating personnel, accessing backup systems and data, and implementing alternative work arrangements. It also outlines the recovery time objectives and strategies for each critical function.

d) IT Disaster Recovery Plan: An IT disaster recovery plan addresses the recovery of technology infrastructure, systems, and data. It includes backup and restoration procedures, off-site storage arrangements, redundancy measures, and testing protocols to ensure the availability and integrity of IT systems.

e) Supply Chain Management: Organizations should assess and address vulnerabilities in their supply chain to ensure continuity of critical supplies, services, and dependencies. This may involve diversifying suppliers, developing alternate sourcing strategies, and establishing communication channels to manage disruptions effectively.

5.4 Plan Implementation: Once the strategies and plans are developed, organizations implement them through:

a) Training and Awareness: Ensuring that employees are aware of their roles and responsibilities during a crisis and are trained on the specific actions outlined in the business continuity plans.

b) Communication: Establishing effective communication channels to disseminate information to employees, stakeholders, customers, and suppliers during a crisis. This includes both internal and external communications to provide timely updates and instructions.

c) Testing and Exercising: Regularly testing and exercising the business continuity plans through simulations, tabletop exercises, or full-scale drills.

This helps identify gaps, improve response capabilities, and familiarize personnel with their roles and procedures.

5.5 Plan Maintenance and Review: Business continuity plans should be regularly reviewed, updated, and tested to ensure their effectiveness. Changes in the organization's structure, operations, or external environment may necessitate modifications to the plans. Ongoing monitoring, evaluation, and feedback mechanisms help identify areas for improvement and address emerging risks.

5.6 Crisis Communication: Effective crisis communication is an essential component of business continuity planning. It involves developing a communication strategy, establishing designated spokespersons, and ensuring consistent, accurate, and timely communication with internal and external stakeholders. Clear communication during a crisis helps manage expectations, maintain trust, and minimize the impact on the organization's reputation.

Business continuity planning is an ongoing process that requires commitment, resources, and active engagement from all levels of the organization. By implementing a robust BCP, organizations can enhance their resilience, minimize disruptions, and ensure the continuity of critical business functions, thereby safeguarding their reputation and maintaining stakeholder confidence.

6. Summary

The chapter delves into various critical aspects of organizational risk management. The chapter begins by discussing the importance of risk identification and assessment, emphasizing the need for a systematic approach to identify potential risks and evaluate their potential impact. It highlights the significance of conducting regular risk assessments to adapt to changing environments and implement effective risk mitigation measures. The chapter also explores the role of internal controls and compliance in mitigating risks and ensuring adherence to laws, regulations, and internal policies. It delves into the components of a robust internal control framework, including control environment, risk assessment, control activities, information and communication, and monitoring. The chapter emphasizes the integration of internal controls and compliance to foster transparency, accountability, and ethical behavior within the organization. Furthermore, it explores fraud prevention strategies and the establishment of whistleblower mechanisms to detect and address fraudulent activities. The chapter concludes with an in-depth discussion on business continuity planning, highlighting the importance of developing strategies and procedures to ensure critical business functions can continue or be swiftly restored during adverse events. It emphasizes the need for risk assessment, strategy development, plan implementation, and regular maintenance to enhance organizational resilience and minimize disruptions.

Thus, this chapter provides a comprehensive overview of risk management and internal controls. It emphasizes the importance of identifying and assessing risks, implementing internal controls and compliance measures, preventing fraud through robust strategies, and establishing whistleblower mechanisms. Additionally, the chapter highlights the significance of business continuity planning to ensure the continuity of critical business functions in the face of disruptions. Overall, this chapter serves as a valuable resource for organizations seeking to enhance their risk management practices, strengthen internal controls, and promote ethical conduct within their operations.

References
1.   AICPA. (2017). Internal Control: A Practical Guide. Wiley.
2.   Crouhy, M., Galai, D., & Mark, R. (2014). The Essentials of Risk Management. McGraw-Hill Education.
3.   Davis, R., & Patterson, M. (2012). Fraud Risk Assessment: Building a Fraud Audit Program. Wiley.
4.   Fraser, J., & Simkins, B. J. (2016). Enterprise Risk Management: Today's Leading Research and Best Practices for Tomorrow's Executives. Wiley.
5.   Greenberg, D. (2017). Enterprise Risk Management: A Common Framework for the Entire Organization. CRC Press.
6.   Hann, R., & Hüneke, S. (2015). Risk Management: Principles and Practices. Routledge.
7.   Institute of Internal Auditors. (2016). Internal Control—Integrated Framework. The IIA Research Foundation.
8.   KPMG. (2019). Internal Control: A Practical Guide. KPMG International.
9.   Lam, J. (2013). Enterprise Risk Management: From Incentives to Controls. Wiley.
10.   Löning, H., & Wischermann, U. (2019). Risk Management and Internal Control: Financial Institutions in the New Era of Regulations. Springer.
11.   Meulbroek, L. K. (2016). Risk Management and Governance: Concepts, Guidelines, and Applications. Oxford University Press.
12.   Mikes, A., & Kaplan, R. S. (2013). Risk Management Framework: A Lab-Based Approach to Securing Information Systems. Wiley.
13.   Moeller, R. R. (2017). COSO Enterprise Risk Management: Establishing Effective Governance, Risk, and Compliance Processes. Wiley.
14.   Pickett, K. H., & Pickett, W. L. (2014). Internal Control Strategies:

A Mid to Small Business Guide. Routledge.

15. Protiviti. (2017). Guide to Enterprise Risk Management: Frequently Asked Questions. Protiviti Inc.

16. PwC. (2019). Risk Assurance: A Comprehensive Guide to Internal Controls. PwC.

17. Salas, A., & Andrikopoulos, P. (2015). Enterprise Risk Management: A Methodology to Assess the Risk of Loss from Internal Fraud. Springer.

18. Sanders, R. (2016). Internal Controls in the Accounting Systems of Small and Medium-Sized Enterprises. Springer.

19. Sharman, P., & McKinlay, A. (2018). Risk Management in Organizations: An Integrated Case Study Approach. Routledge.

20. Thamhain, H. J., & Wilemon, D. (2019). Risk Management Handbook for Health Care Organizations. John Wiley & Sons.

CHAPTER 7
CORPORATE GOVERNANCE AND STAKEHOLDERS
Ms. Gurpreet Kaur[7]

Chapter Abstract

This chapter explores the intricate relationship between corporate governance and stakeholders within the business landscape. It delves into four key stakeholder groups - employees, customers, suppliers, and the community - and examines how effective corporate governance practices can foster positive stakeholder management and drive organizational success.

The chapter begins by examining the significance of employees as critical stakeholders and the impact of employment practices on corporate governance. It delves into various aspects of employment, including recruitment, training, performance evaluation, and remuneration, emphasizing the need for transparent and fair practices aligned with strategic objectives. The chapter also highlights the importance of fostering employee engagement, participation, and well-being within the governance framework.

Moving on to customers, the chapter explores the role of corporate governance in ensuring consumer protection and ethical business practices. It discusses the importance of transparency, accountability, and fair treatment of customers, focusing on areas such as product information, pricing practices, and complaint handling mechanisms. The chapter emphasizes the need to build trust, maintain high ethical standards, and safeguard customer data and privacy in an increasingly digital landscape.

Next, the chapter examines the relationship between corporate governance and suppliers, with a specific focus on supply chain governance. It discusses the complexities of modern supply chains and emphasizes the

---

[7] Assistant Professor, School of Management Studies, CT University, Ludhiana

significance of responsible sourcing, supplier selection, and ethical supply chain practices within the governance framework. The chapter also highlights the importance of sustainability considerations, including environmental impact and resource management, for effective supply chain governance.

Lastly, the chapter explores the role of corporate governance in community engagement and social responsibility. It discusses the importance of businesses actively engaging with the communities in which they operate, contributing to social and environmental well-being, and addressing relevant challenges. The chapter emphasizes the need for governance structures that foster ethical behavior, compliance with laws and regulations, and the integration of environmental, social, and governance (ESG) factors into business strategies.

Overall, this chapter underscores the crucial relationship between corporate governance and stakeholders. By examining employees, customers, suppliers, and community engagement, it highlights how effective governance practices can contribute to sustainable and responsible business conduct, benefiting both the organization and its stakeholders.

1. Employees and Employment Practices

In the realm of corporate governance, employees play a critical role as key stakeholders. They are not only essential to the day-to-day operations of a company but also contribute to its long-term success. This section focuses on the relationship between corporate governance and employees, examining the significance of employment practices and their impact on the overall organizational performance.

Effective corporate governance ensures that the interests of employees are protected and their rights are upheld. Companies must establish transparent and fair employment practices, including recruitment, training, performance evaluation, and remuneration. These practices should be aligned with the company's strategic objectives and values while promoting a positive and inclusive work environment.

Furthermore, corporate governance should promote employee engagement and participation in decision-making processes. This can be achieved through the establishment of mechanisms such as employee representation on the board of directors or through regular communication channels that enable employees to provide feedback and contribute to the company's decision-making.

In addition to compliance with labor laws and regulations, corporate governance should prioritize the health and safety of employees. This includes providing a safe working environment, adequate training, and clear protocols for addressing occupational hazards. Moreover, governance structures should support the protection of employees' well-being, both physical and mental, fostering work-life balance and addressing issues such as workplace harassment or discrimination.

Overall, a robust corporate governance framework acknowledges the importance of employees as stakeholders and aims to create a culture that values their contributions, protects their rights, and enables their growth and development within the organization.

2. Customers and Consumer Protection

Customers are vital stakeholders for any business, and their interests should be a central focus of corporate governance practices. Consumer protection is an essential aspect of effective governance, ensuring that companies prioritize the satisfaction and well-being of their customers while maintaining high ethical standards.

Corporate governance should encompass policies and procedures that promote transparency and accountability in all customer interactions. This includes clear communication of product or service features, fair pricing practices, and protection against deceptive advertising or unfair contractual terms. Moreover, companies should establish effective complaint handling mechanisms, allowing customers to voice their concerns and seek redress when necessary.

Furthermore, governance frameworks should encourage ethical marketing practices that avoid manipulative or misleading tactics. Companies should strive to build trust and long-term relationships with their customers, rather than focusing solely on short-term profit maximization. This can be achieved through initiatives such as customer engagement programs, loyalty schemes, and a commitment to delivering high-quality products or services.

Corporate governance should also address the protection of customer data and privacy. With the increasing digitalization of businesses, companies must adopt robust cybersecurity measures to safeguard customer information from unauthorized access or breaches. Compliance with data protection laws and regulations should be a priority, with clear policies on data collection, storage, and usage.

By prioritizing customer satisfaction, trust, and data protection, effective corporate governance promotes long-term success and sustainability for businesses.

3. Suppliers and Supply Chain Governance

In today's interconnected global economy, supply chains have become complex and geographically dispersed. Suppliers play a critical role in the success of a company, making supply chain governance an integral part of corporate governance. This section explores the relationship between corporate governance and suppliers, emphasizing the importance of ethical and sustainable supply chain practices.

Corporate governance should encompass policies and procedures that promote responsible sourcing and supplier selection. Companies should establish clear criteria for supplier evaluation, taking into account factors such as quality, reliability, ethical standards, and environmental sustainability. Transparency in supplier selection processes ensures fair competition and promotes accountability.

To ensure ethical practices throughout the supply chain, companies should establish supplier codes of conduct that outline the expected standards of behavior. These codes should cover areas such as labor rights, environmental impact, and anti-corruption measures. Regular monitoring and auditing of suppliers can help ensure compliance with these standards.

Furthermore, corporate governance should encourage collaboration and long-term relationships with suppliers based on trust and mutual benefit. Companies should engage in open and transparent communication with suppliers, fostering a partnership approach that promotes shared goals and values. This can include initiatives such as capacity building programs for suppliers or joint efforts to address sustainability challenges.

Supply chain governance should also address environmental sustainability, promoting practices that minimize waste, reduce carbon footprint, and support responsible resource management. This can involve initiatives such as sustainable sourcing, waste reduction programs, or the adoption of renewable energy sources.

Overall, effective supply chain governance within the framework of corporate governance promotes ethical supplier relationships, fosters sustainability, and mitigates risks associated with supply chain disruptions.

4. Community Engagement and Social Responsibility

Beyond the boundaries of a company, corporate governance extends to the communities in which businesses operate. Community engagement and social responsibility are essential aspects of effective governance, ensuring that companies contribute positively to society and address the interests of the broader community.

Corporate governance should incorporate policies and practices that foster community engagement. This includes initiatives such as partnerships with local organizations, sponsorship of community events, or volunteering programs that encourage employees' involvement in community activities. By actively participating in community development, companies can establish positive relationships, build trust, and enhance their reputation.

Moreover, social responsibility should be ingrained in a company's strategic objectives and decision-making processes. This can involve integrating environmental, social, and governance (ESG) factors into business strategies, considering the impact of operations on the environment and society. By adopting sustainable practices, companies can minimize negative externalities and contribute to the well-being of communities.

In addition, effective governance should address corporate philanthropy and charitable initiatives. Companies can establish corporate foundations or allocate resources to support projects or organizations that address social or environmental challenges. By aligning philanthropic efforts with the company's core values and mission, corporate governance ensures that these initiatives are purposeful and impactful.

Lastly, corporate governance should prioritize ethical behavior and compliance with laws and regulations that promote social responsibility. This includes anti-corruption measures, fair competition practices, and adherence to labor and human rights standards.

In summary, community engagement and social responsibility are integral to effective corporate governance. By considering the broader impact of their actions and engaging with communities, companies can contribute to sustainable development and create shared value for all stakeholders.

5. Summary

In this chapter, the intricate relationship between corporate governance and stakeholders is explored. The chapter begins by emphasizing the significance of employees as key stakeholders and examines the impact of employment practices on corporate governance. It delves into various aspects such as recruitment, training, performance evaluation, and remuneration, emphasizing the need for fairness, transparency, and employee engagement. The chapter also highlights the importance of creating a positive work environment that values employee well-being and fosters their participation in decision-making processes.

Moving on, the chapter focuses on customers as stakeholders and discusses the role of corporate governance in ensuring consumer protection. It highlights the importance of transparency, accountability, and fair treatment of customers. The chapter emphasizes the need for ethical business practices, including clear communication, fair pricing, and effective complaint handling mechanisms. It also addresses the importance of building trust, maintaining high ethical standards, and safeguarding customer data and privacy.

The chapter then delves into the relationship between corporate governance and suppliers, with a focus on supply chain governance. It emphasizes the need for responsible sourcing, supplier selection, and ethical supply chain practices. The chapter discusses the complexities of modern supply chains and highlights the significance of sustainability considerations, such as environmental impact and resource management.

Lastly, the chapter explores the role of corporate governance in community engagement and social responsibility. It emphasizes the importance of businesses actively engaging with the communities in which they operate and addressing social and environmental challenges. The chapter highlights the need for ethical behavior, compliance with laws and regulations, and the integration of environmental, social, and governance (ESG) factors into business strategies.

Overall, this chapter underscores the crucial relationship between corporate governance and stakeholders. It highlights the importance of effective governance practices in managing employees, protecting customers, fostering responsible supplier relationships, and engaging with the community. By prioritizing stakeholder interests, businesses can enhance their sustainability and long-term success.

References
1.   Agle, B. R., Mitchell, R. K., & Sonnenfeld, J. A. (1999). Who matters to CEOs? An investigation of stakeholder attributes and salience, corporate performance, and CEO values. Academy of Management Journal, 42(5), 507-525.
2.   Blair, M. M. (1995). Ownership and control: Rethinking corporate governance for the twenty-first century. Brookings Institution Press.
3.   Clarkson, M. B. (1995). A stakeholder framework for analyzing and evaluating corporate social performance. Academy of Management Review, 20(1), 92-117.
4.   Davis, J. H., Schoorman, F. D., & Donaldson, L. (1997). Toward a stewardship theory of management. Academy of Management Review, 22(1), 20-47.
5.   Donaldson, T., & Preston, L. E. (1995). The stakeholder theory of the corporation: Concepts, evidence, and implications. Academy of Management Review, 20(1), 65-91.
6.   Freeman, R. E. (1984). Strategic management: A stakeholder approach. Pitman.
7.   Freeman, R. E., Harrison, J. S., Wicks, A. C., Parmar, B. L., & De Colle, S. (2010). Stakeholder theory: The state of the art. Cambridge University Press.
8.   Hillman, A. J., & Keim, G. D. (2001). Shareholder value, stakeholder management, and social issues: What's the bottom line? Strategic Management Journal, 22(2), 125-139.
9.   Jensen, M. C., & Meckling, W. H. (1976). Theory of the firm: Managerial behavior, agency costs, and ownership structure. Journal of Financial Economics, 3(4), 305-360.
10.   Jones, T. M. (1995). Instrumental stakeholder theory: A synthesis of ethics and economics. Academy of Management Review, 20(2), 404-437.
11.   Kiel, G. C., & Nicholson, G. J. (2003). Board composition and corporate performance: How the Australian experience informs contrasting theories of corporate governance. Corporate Governance: An International Review, 11(3), 189-205.

12. Lazonick, W. (1991). Business organization and the myth of the market economy. Cambridge University Press.

13. Monks, R. A. G., & Minow, N. (2011). Corporate governance. John Wiley & Sons.

14. Parmar, B. L., Freeman, R. E., Harrison, J. S., Wicks, A. C., Purnell, L., & De Colle, S. (2010). Stakeholder theory: The state of the art. Academy of Management Annals, 4(1), 403-445.

15. Pearce, J. A., & Zahra, S. A. (1991). The relative power of CEOs and boards of directors: Associations with corporate performance. Strategic Management Journal, 12(2), 135-153.

16. Pfeffer, J., & Salancik, G. R. (1978). The external control of organizations: A resource dependence perspective. Harper & Row.

17. Roberts, J. (2004). The modern firm: Organizational design for performance and growth. Oxford University Press.

18. Roberts, P. W., & Dowling, G. R. (2002). Corporate reputation and sustained superior financial performance. Strategic Management Journal, 23(12), 1077-1093.

19. Rupp, D. E., Ganapathi, J., Aguilera, R. V., & Williams, C. A. (2006). Employee reactions to corporate social responsibility: An organizational justice framework. Journal of Organizational Behavior, 27(4), 537-543.

20. Sethi, S. P., & Falbe, C. M. (1987). Corporate social performance and corporate financial performance: A research synthesis. International Association for Business and Society, 2(1), 33-44.

21. Solomon, J. (2007). Corporate governance and accountability. John Wiley & Sons.

22. Stout, L. A. (2012). The shareholder value myth: How putting shareholders first harms investors, corporations, and the public. Berrett-Koehler Publishers.

23. Tricker, R. I. (2015). Corporate governance: Principles, policies, and practices. Oxford University Press.

24. Ullmann, A. A. (1985). Data in search of a theory: A critical examination of the relationships among social performance, social disclosure, and economic performance of US firms. Academy of Management Review, 10(3), 540-557.

25. Waddock, S. A., & Graves, S. B. (1997). The corporate social performance-financial performance link. Strategic Management Journal, 18(4), 303-319.

CHAPTER 8
CORPORATE GOVERNANCE PRACTICES IN INDIA
Ms. Riddhie Priya[8]

Chapter Abstract

Corporate governance plays a crucial role in the functioning and sustainability of companies, ensuring transparency, accountability, and ethical practices. In recent years, India has made significant strides in enhancing its corporate governance practices through legislative reforms, regulatory frameworks, and voluntary initiatives. This chapter provides an overview of the corporate governance landscape in India, highlighting key practices, case studies, ratings, rankings, challenges, and future directions.

1. Case Studies and Best Practices

In this section, we will explore some case studies and best practices in corporate governance in India. These examples highlight companies that have demonstrated exemplary governance practices and can serve as models for others to follow.

Case Study 1: Infosys Limited

Infosys Limited, a leading Indian multinational corporation in the IT industry, is widely recognized for its robust corporate governance practices. The company has established a strong governance framework that prioritizes transparency, accountability, and stakeholder engagement.

Infosys has a board of directors comprising a majority of independent directors, ensuring unbiased decision-making and effective oversight. The

---

[8] Assistant Professor, School of Management Studies, CT University, Ludhiana

board is responsible for setting the company's strategic direction, monitoring performance, and upholding ethical standards. Additionally, Infosys has established various committees, such as the Audit Committee, Nomination and Remuneration Committee, and Risk Management Committee, to address specific governance areas.

The company follows a policy of timely and transparent disclosure of financial information and operational performance. Infosys publishes quarterly and annual reports, providing shareholders and stakeholders with comprehensive information about the company's financial health, risk management, and sustainability initiatives.

Moreover, Infosys has implemented strong internal controls and risk management mechanisms to safeguard the interests of shareholders. The company regularly conducts internal audits to assess compliance with policies, identify risks, and ensure effective control systems.

Case Study 2: Larsen & Toubro Limited

Larsen & Toubro Limited (L&T), a diversified Indian engineering and construction conglomerate, has established itself as a benchmark for corporate governance in the country. The company has adopted several best practices that promote transparency, ethical conduct, and shareholder value.

L&T has a well-structured board of directors, comprising a balanced mix of executive and independent directors. The board is responsible for strategic decision-making, risk oversight, and ensuring compliance with regulatory requirements. Independent directors play a crucial role in providing objective advice, protecting minority shareholders' interests, and ensuring effective governance.

The company has implemented a comprehensive code of conduct that outlines ethical standards and guides employee behavior. L&T encourages a culture of integrity, fairness, and transparency across all levels of the organization. It also promotes a whistleblower policy that allows employees to report unethical practices without fear of reprisal.

L&T has established strong internal control systems, including risk management processes and internal audits, to identify and mitigate potential risks. The company emphasizes sustainable practices and regularly discloses its environmental, social, and governance initiatives in its annual sustainability reports.

Case Study 3: Tata Group

The Tata Group, one of India's largest conglomerates, has long been regarded as a pioneer of good corporate governance in the country. Under the leadership of Ratan Tata, the group implemented several measures to enhance transparency and accountability. These include appointing a majority of independent directors on its boards, establishing robust audit committees, and adopting strict internal control mechanisms. Additionally, the Tata Group has emphasized ethical conduct, sustainability, and social responsibility, which are reflected in its policies and initiatives. The group's commitment to corporate governance has helped it build trust among stakeholders and maintain its reputation.

Best Practices:

1.   Independent Directors: Companies should strive to have a majority of independent directors on their boards to ensure unbiased decision-making and effective oversight.

2.   Board Committees: Establishing dedicated committees, such as audit committees, remuneration committees, and risk management committees, can enhance governance effectiveness and focus on specific areas of concern.

3.   Transparent Disclosure: Companies should provide timely and comprehensive disclosures of financial information, risk factors, and corporate governance practices to shareholders and stakeholders.

4.   Ethics and Code of Conduct: Adopting and enforcing a robust code of conduct that emphasizes ethical behavior, integrity, and compliance with legal and regulatory requirements.

5.   Shareholder Engagement: Encouraging shareholder participation through regular communication, shareholder meetings, and providing mechanisms for shareholders to express their views and concerns.

6.   Risk Management: Implementing robust risk management processes, internal controls, and internal audits to identify and mitigate risks that may impact the company's performance and reputation.

These case studies and best practices illustrate the importance of strong corporate governance in building trust, protecting shareholder interests, and ensuring long-term sustainability. By adopting these practices, companies in India can strengthen their governance frameworks and contribute to a healthy and transparent business environment.

2. Corporate Governance Ratings and Rankings

In this section, we will delve into corporate governance ratings and rankings in India. These assessments provide valuable insights into the governance practices of companies and help investors and stakeholders make informed decisions. Several organizations and institutions in India evaluate and rank companies based on their adherence to corporate governance principles.

2.1 National Stock Exchange (NSE) Corporate Governance Score: The National Stock Exchange (NSE) assesses the corporate governance practices of companies listed on its platform through the NSE's Corporate Governance Score. The score evaluates companies based on various parameters, including board structure, composition, independence, disclosure practices, and shareholder rights. The assessment aims to encourage companies to enhance their governance practices and promote transparency and accountability.

2.2 Bombay Stock Exchange (BSE) Corporate Governance and Compliance Rating: The Bombay Stock Exchange (BSE) evaluates companies' corporate governance practices through its Corporate Governance and Compliance Rating (CGCR). The CGCR assesses companies based on factors such as board composition, audit committees, related-party transactions, financial disclosures, and risk management. The rating helps investors assess the level of corporate governance compliance in a company.

2.3 Securities and Exchange Board of India (SEBI) Corporate Governance Norms: The Securities and Exchange Board of India (SEBI), the regulatory body for securities markets in India, has introduced various corporate governance norms. These norms encompass board composition, independent directors, audit committees, financial disclosures, and related-party transactions. Companies are required to comply with SEBI's guidelines and regulations, which are periodically updated to align with international best practices.

2.4 Institutional Investor Advisory Services (IiAS) Score: Institutional Investor Advisory Services (IiAS) is an independent proxy advisory firm that assesses companies' corporate governance practices. IiAS evaluates companies based on parameters such as board independence, audit committee effectiveness, executive compensation, and shareholder rights. The IiAS score provides investors with an assessment of the governance practices of listed companies.

2.5 Confederation of Indian Industry (CII) Governance Rating: The Confederation of Indian Industry (CII) has developed a governance rating framework to assess the governance practices of Indian companies. The rating evaluates companies based on criteria such as board composition, disclosure practices, risk management, and stakeholder engagement. The CII governance rating aims to promote best practices in corporate governance and recognize companies with high governance standards.

These ratings and rankings serve as important tools for investors, regulators, and stakeholders to evaluate companies' corporate governance practices. They create benchmarks for companies to improve their governance structures, enhance transparency, and build investor confidence. Additionally, the ratings foster healthy competition among companies to adopt and maintain good corporate governance practices.

It is important to note that ratings and rankings are subjective assessments based on specific criteria. Investors and stakeholders should consider multiple sources of information and conduct their own due diligence when evaluating companies for investment or engagement.

3. Challenges and Future Directions

In this section, we will discuss the challenges faced by corporate governance in India and explore future directions to further strengthen governance practices.

3.1 Challenges

1.   Related-Party Transactions: One of the significant challenges in corporate governance is related-party transactions. These transactions involve dealings between a company and its affiliates or entities with close relationships to board members or key executives. It can create conflicts of interest and raise concerns about fairness and transparency.

2.   Board Composition and Independence: Ensuring a diverse and independent board of directors remains a challenge. Achieving gender diversity and representation from different backgrounds and expertise is crucial for effective decision-making and avoiding groupthink.

3.   Shareholder Activism and Protection: India has witnessed an increasing trend of shareholder activism. Ensuring protection and empowerment of minority shareholders and enhancing their rights are important for a fair and inclusive corporate governance ecosystem.

4.   Enforcement and Compliance: While regulations and guidelines exist to promote good governance, effective enforcement remains a challenge. Ensuring compliance by companies of all sizes, especially smaller enterprises, requires robust monitoring mechanisms.

5.   Sustainability and ESG Integration: Integrating environmental, social, and governance (ESG) factors into corporate governance frameworks is gaining importance. Companies need to address ESG risks and opportunities and align their governance practices with sustainable development goals.

3.2 Future Directions

1.   Strengthening Regulatory Frameworks: Continual refinement and strengthening of corporate governance regulations is necessary to keep pace with evolving business dynamics, emerging risks, and global best practices. Regular updates and reforms should be undertaken to ensure relevance and effectiveness.

2.   Investor Education and Awareness: Enhancing investor education and awareness about corporate governance practices and their impact on long-term value creation is vital. Educated investors can make informed decisions, actively participate in shareholder meetings, and hold companies accountable.

3.   Technology and Governance: Exploring the integration of technology in corporate governance can improve transparency, efficiency, and accountability. Technologies such as blockchain, artificial intelligence, and data analytics can streamline compliance, enhance shareholder engagement, and facilitate secure and transparent voting processes.

4.   ESG Integration: Promoting the integration of ESG factors into corporate governance frameworks is essential for sustainable business practices. Encouraging companies to report on their ESG performance and aligning governance practices with sustainability goals will contribute to long-term value creation.

5.   Whistleblower   Protection   and   Reporting   Mechanisms: Strengthening whistleblower protection mechanisms and establishing confidential reporting channels can encourage employees and stakeholders to report unethical behavior without fear of retaliation. It fosters a culture of accountability and transparency within organizations.

6.   Strengthening Board Independence and Diversity: Encouraging gender diversity and diverse representation on corporate boards is critical. Regulatory measures, voluntary initiatives, and awareness campaigns can facilitate the appointment of independent directors and diverse board compositions.

7.   Collaboration and Engagement: Collaboration between regulators, industry associations, companies, and investors is key to promoting effective corporate governance practices. Regular dialogue, sharing of best practices, and collective efforts can drive positive change.

By addressing these challenges and embracing future directions, India can continue to enhance its corporate governance practices. A strong governance framework fosters trust, attracts investments, and promotes sustainable growth, benefiting companies, investors, and the overall economy.

4. Summary

Over the years, India has made remarkable progress in enhancing corporate governance practices. The implementation of case study-based best practices, such as those demonstrated by companies like Infosys and Larsen & Toubro, has set a benchmark for transparency, accountability, and ethical conduct. These case studies showcase the significance of independent directors, robust internal control mechanisms, and timely and transparent disclosures in fostering good corporate governance. By adopting and implementing these best practices, Indian companies are instilling confidence in their stakeholders, attracting investments, and strengthening their reputation.

Furthermore, the establishment of rating systems by organizations like the NSE, BSE, and SEBI has been instrumental in assessing and benchmarking corporate governance practices in India. These ratings and rankings provide investors with valuable insights into the governance structures and practices of companies. They act as a catalyst for companies to improve their governance frameworks and promote healthy competition among them. Additionally, the focus on regulatory reforms, such as those introduced by SEBI, in conjunction with investor education initiatives, helps raise awareness about the importance of corporate governance and empowers stakeholders to actively participate in governance processes. The integration of sustainable governance practices, including the consideration of ESG factors, demonstrates India's commitment to aligning corporate governance with broader sustainability goals.

Looking ahead, continued emphasis on regulatory reforms will play a pivotal role in strengthening corporate governance in India. Regular updates and enhancements to the existing frameworks will ensure they remain effective in addressing emerging challenges and keeping pace with evolving business dynamics. Moreover, promoting investor education and awareness programs will empower shareholders to make informed decisions and actively engage in governance processes. By fostering a culture of transparency, accountability, and ethical conduct, India can further enhance its position in the global corporate governance arena, attract investments, and build a resilient and sustainable business ecosystem.

References
1.   Bala, S. (2019). Corporate Governance in India: An Overview. Springer.
2.   Bandyopadhyay, A., & Sinha, A. (Eds.). (2017). Handbook of Research on Corporate Governance in Banking and Financial Institutions. IGI Global.
3.   Bhattacharyya, S., & Mittal, S. (2018). Corporate Governance in India: Change and Continuity. Sage Publications.
4.   BSE (Bombay Stock Exchange). (2021). Corporate Governance and Compliance Rating. Retrieved from https://www.bseindia.com/corporates/List-of-CG-and-CR-Graded-Companies/12878/1e9d2f1a-ec01-4a7f-9630-161b319ce8e7
5.   Business Standard. (2022). Infosys. Retrieved from https://www.business-standard.com/company/infosys-10955/information/company-history
6.   CII (Confederation of Indian Industry). (2019). Code for Responsible Business. Retrieved from

https://www.cii.in/CIIResponsibleBusiness/pages/Code

7.   IiAS (Institutional Investor Advisory Services). (2022). India Proxy Season 2022. Retrieved from https://www.iiasadvisory.com/research-2022/india-proxy-season-2022.html

8.   Jindal, S. (2017). Corporate Governance Practices in India: A Critical Analysis. Springer.

9.   Khurana, I. K., & Batra, G. S. (2019). Corporate Governance in India: An Integrative Perspective. Oxford University Press.

10.   Kotak Committee on Corporate Governance. (2017). Report on Corporate   Governance.   Retrieved   from https://www.sebi.gov.in/sebi_data/attachdocs/1489535326151.pdf

11.   Law   Commission   of   India.   (2017).   Report   on   Corporate Governance   and   Shareholder   Activism.   Retrieved   from http://www.lawcommissionofindia.nic.in/reports/Report272.pdf

12.   Malhotra, D. K., & Singh, S. (2018). Corporate Governance in India: Past, Present, and Future. Sage Publications.

13.   NSE (National Stock Exchange). (2022). Corporate Governance. Retrieved from https://www.nseindia.com/invest/resources/corporate-governance

14.   Ramanna, K., & Lount, J. (2018). Corporate Governance in India. Harvard Business School Case 118-034.

15.   SEBI (Securities and Exchange Board of India). (2018). SEBI (Listing Obligations and Disclosure Requirements) Regulations, 2015. Retrieved from https://www.sebi.gov.in/legal/regulations/dec-2015/sebi-listing-obligations-and-disclosure-requirements-regulations-2015-last-amended-on-july-12-2021_26139.html

16.   SEBI (Securities and Exchange Board of India). (2020). SEBI Circular on COVID-19 Related Disclosures by Listed Entities. Retrieved from   https://www.sebi.gov.in/legal/circulars/mar-2020/sebi-circular-on-covid-19-related-disclosures-by-listed-entities_46452.html

17.   Sharma, P., & Chandra, A. (2019). Corporate Governance in India: An Exploration. Routledge.

18.   Srinivasan, R. (2019). Corporate Governance: Principles, Policies, and Practices. Oxford University Press.

19.   Tandon, B., & Gupta, A. (2021). Corporate Governance: Theory and Practice. Pearson Education India.

20.   Verma, S. K., & Sharma, V. (2019). Corporate Governance Practices and Financial Performance: An Empirical Study of Indian Companies. Palgrave Macmillan.

ABOUT THE AUTHOR

Dr. Kangan Sayal is an accomplished academic and researcher in the domain of management. She completed her Ph.D. in Management from Thapar University, Patiala where she specialized in management. With her dedication and passion for research, she has made significant contributions to the field of management through her published research articles in prestigious journals. Currently, she holds the position of Assistant Professor at the School of Management Studies, CT University in Ludhiana.

Dr. Navdeep Kaur is an associate professor at the School of Management Studies, CT University in Ludhiana.

Dr. Kawal Nain Singh is an associate professor at the School of Management Studies, CT University in Ludhiana.

Dr. Nikhil Monga is a professor and dean at the School of Management Studies, CT University in Ludhiana.

Ms. Lovejit Kaur is an assistant professor at the School of Management Studies, CT University in Ludhiana.

Ms. Gurpreet Kaur is an assistant professor at the School of Management Studies, CT University in Ludhiana.

Ms. Riddhie Priya is an assistant professor at the School of Management Studies, CT University in Ludhiana.

Printed in Dunstable, United Kingdom